THE RAWLINSONS
from
FURNESS FELLS

David A Jackson

Published in 2023 by David A Jackson

© Copyright David A Jackson

ISBN: 978-1-913898-78-6

Cover and Book interior Design by Russell Holden
www.pixeltweakspublications.com

Pixel Tweaks Publications
SELF PUBLISHING MADE SIMPLE

A Catalogue record for this book is
available from the British Library.

ACKNOWLEDGMENTS

I have had a lot of help with this book. First from Russell Holden of Pixel Tweaks who kindly takes the pain out of self publishing. Then to Sue Benson and Selina Kendall of Barrow Record Office, to the staff of Lancashire Record Office at Preston, to the staff of Ulverston Library, to the Lancaster Maritime Museum, to Mishka Sinha for use of her blog on Richard Rawlinson and for advice on sources, to Michael Reirdon of St John's College Oxford for access to the records of Richard Rawlinson the antiquary, to Alice Milea of the Oxford University Archives for access to their material on Richard Rawlinson. To the staff of Carlisle Record Office. To Stephen Freeth the archivist of The Vintners Company, to the staff at the Public Record Office Kew, to the staff at the Greater London Record Office and the staff of the Guildhall Library, Andrew Parratt curator Government Art Collection, Joanne Heather of Hawkshead Museum and staff of King Edward School Witley. Bernard and Elizabeth Ellis for help with transport and Elizabeth Ellis for certain photographs.I appreciate further help from Robert Sutton book seller and Peter Lowe antiquarian for reading the manuscript. Any surviving mistakes are mine.

CONTENTS

Contents

INTRODUCTION

I first came across the Rawlinsons when I was researching Swarthmoor Hall and its People. Thomas Rawlinson, who became a Quaker managed Force Forge for the Fell sisters and later bought it from them. Richard Rawlinson appears as an agent in the vast indenture tripartite in which Daniel Abraham bought out the interest of all other members of the Fell family including Charles who had attained his majority in Swarthmoor Hall. Then there was Abigail Rawlinson of Lancaster, who married William Lindow after his return from Grenada. I then found out that all these people were connected to the same extensive and ramifying family. There are two main branches. One which I call the Graythwaite group from their eventual principal residence starting as far as I can see with Robert Rawlinson of Greenhead Gill and Colton Mill fl 1484. The other originated in Grizedale of which Thomas Rawlinson of Grizedale (will proved 1591) is the earliest for whom the surviving records give attestation.

The two families persistently addressed each other as cousin. John Rawlinson of Hullater of the Grizedale branch, acted as local land agent in Furness for John Rawlinson, secretary to the Master of the Rolls in London, of the Graythwaite branch. There are a number of letters between them where each calling the other cousin despite the difference in social status. Christopher Rawlinson of Cark last of that male line left his lands to Richard Rawlinson the antiquary in preference to much closer relations in the female line. Christopher belonged to the Graythwaite branch and Richard to the Grizedale branch . The common ancestor, assuming there was one would be 13th or early 14th century not long after surnames became established.

Both Grizedale and Graythwaite are in the chapelry of Satterthwaite. In the extant assessments for relief of the poor, 1652-1707 both sets of Rawlinsons are assessed the Graythwaite branch for rather more than the Grizedale branch who are assessed despite being resident in London - both Daniel and his son Sir Thomas paying the assessment: John Rawlinson of the Rolls office is also assessed for a forge as is the elder Abraham Rawlinson . The other substantial assessments are those of the Sandys who pay the same as Graythwaite or sometimes slightly more. Another notable assessment in 1652 is for Thomas Fell esquire who is asked for a fee farm at Parkamoor and for wood rents at Satterthwaite, Grizedale, Dale Park and Graythwaite. He is probably Judge Fell of Swarthmoor.

There are some pedigrees in existence, Dugdale did one showing the descent of the Cark branch. It also appears in Fr West's "Antiquities of Furness" and is said to have been drawn up by Christopher as a young man. It seems to be accurate as far as it goes. For the Grizedale family Richard the antiquarian produced one reproduced by Brian Enright in his D Phil on Richard and his writings and collection. This gives the Thomas who died 1591 a father called Robert and a grandfather called Robert but without supporting evidence. There is also Joseph Foster a voluminous producer of North country pedigrees who is not always reliable. He makes the Thomas Rawlinson who married Susanna Steinberger in 1616 a younger son of the Greenhead line. This is false This Thomas is the son of a Robert of Grizedale and the grandson of Thomas who died in 1591 as evidenced by the wills of the elder Thomas, Margaret his wife and Robert their son. Foster's mistake was pointed out by George Browne of Troutbeck writing to Henry Swainson Cowper author of History of Hawkshead published in 1899. He cited the wills of the Robert and the earlier Thomas. Pedigrees without supporting facts should be viewed with caution. If there is evidence from wills, deeds, parish registers where extant, surviving family letters, contemporary public announcements one can construct a reasonably reliable pedigree. I shall insert table pedigrees at various points in the text. List pedigrees which can accommodate more information will be appendices. Not all the persons in the list pedigrees will appear in the text.

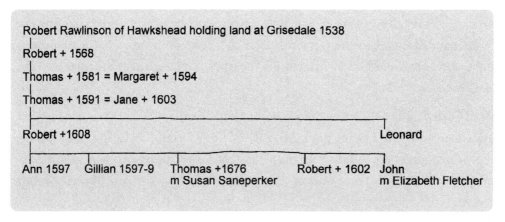

Robert Rawlinson of Hawkshead holding land at Grisedale 1538

Robert + 1568

Thomas + 1581 = Margaret + 1594

Thomas + 1591 = Jane + 1603

Robert +1608   Leonard

Ann 1597   Gillian 1597-9   Thomas +1676   Robert + 1602   John
                 m Susan Saneperker   m Elizabeth Fletcher

Brian Enrights pedigree of Rawlinson of Grizedale

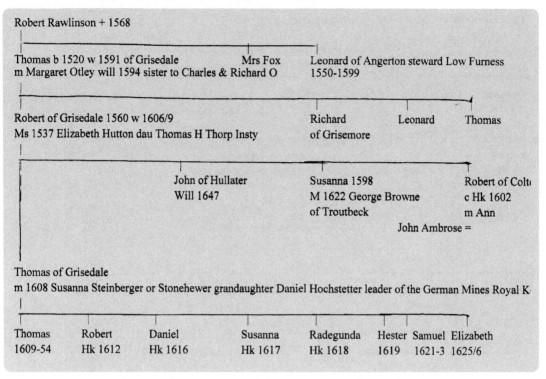

Rawlinson of Grizedale using wills and other documents

The Grizedale branch produces two subgroups. The Angerton family start with Leonard a younger brother of Thomas will 1591. They also lived at Marsh Grange, Dalton, Rampside. Robert of Grizedale son of one Thomas and father of another had a younger son John of Hullater who founds that branch. Robert of Grizedale in a deed of 1584 claimed his father Thomas was seized of a tenement in Colton called Hallater. Further in 1647 Richard Rawlinson of Hullater grants half of Hullater to his son Robert. John Rawlinson of Hullater pays the subsidy in 1547. It is possible that the John Rawlinson bailiff who pays a subsidy at Colton in 1598 is of Hullater

Rawlinson of Hullater

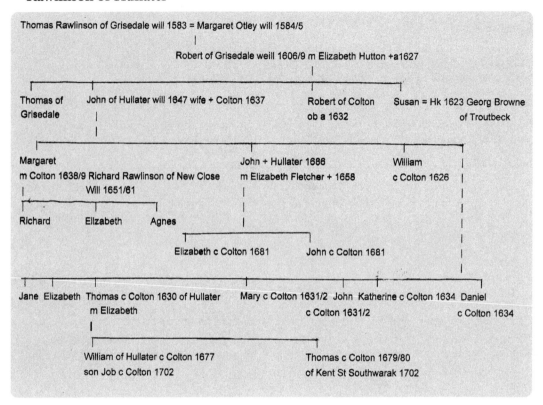

The Graythwaite branch acquired Cark Hall, Mireside Cartmell, Tottlebank and Graythwaite. Afterwards one branch moved to Lancaster and lived at Grassyards.

That family moved South to Chadlington in Oxfordshire.

THE EARLY RAWLINSONS

It is claimed that two Rawlinsons fought at the Battle of Agincourt on 25th October 1415 and that the Rawlinson who was one of the later Abbots of Furness was one of the family, but no proof for either statement is offered.

I intend to write about various members of the family whose lives seem to have been particularly interesting starting with Leonard Rawlinson of Angerton and finishing with Henry Seymour Rawlinson; General Lord Rawlinson who fought in World War One.

Thomas Rawlinson (will proved 1591) had a sister Mrs Foxe, a brother Leonard with children Thomas William and Agnes, a wife Margaret and sons Robert and Leonard. Of these brother Leonard is Leonard Rawlinson of Angerton died 1599 whom we will see later, Wife Margaret leaves a will in 1595 mentions son Robert and grandson Thomas, two brothers called Otley.

Leonard in his will mentions a nephew Robert Rawlinson, a wife Agnes and children John, Robert, Leonard, Thomas and Jane wife of John Benham . The son Robert of Grizedale in his will 1606/9 mentions his wife Elizabeth, a brother Thomas, a brother Richard who was to have Grysemore (sic) and children Elynor (sic), Thomas, John, Margaret, Elizabeth and Robert, Thomas is to inherit Grizedale, John Hullater and Robert land at Colton. Robert's widow Ann marries John Ambrose of Lowick in 1632. There is another girl Susan who marries George Browne of Troutbeck in 1623. This George Browne built Townsend at Troutbeck now owned by the National Trust. The previously mentioned George Browne is a descendant of his and the last of the family to live at Troutbeck. Elizabeth, wife of Robert Rawlinson of Grizedale was the daughter of Thomas Hutton of Thorpinsty.

James VI sold manors and manorial incidents to London speculators. Two of them were William Whitmore and George Whitmore. They sold by indenture 1614 property rights at Grizedale to Thomas Rawlinson of Grizedale gentleman, Thomas Rawlinson of Graythwaite gentleman, John Sawrey and Henry Kirkby of Satterthwaite. In 1615 they sold again this time to Thomas Rawlinson (without saying which) John Sawrey and Henry Kirkby. However in 1617 Thomas Rawlinson, John Sawrey and Henry Kirby make a transfer to Thomas Rawlinson of Grizedale. So presumably the unplaced Thomas Rawlinson was of Graythwaite. Thomas's father Robert acquired rights by Deed Poll from Miles Frearson of Grizedale.

Robert Rawlinson of Greenhead Gill and Colton Mill in Colton parish was alive in 1484. He had two sons John and William. The younger son William lived in Henry VIII's reign and married in 1509 a daughter of Robert Benson of Low Wray and Skelwith and possibly also Loughrigg. He had two sons John and William.

William married Katherine Sawrey and was of Tottlebank and is featured below. John married a daughter of Miles Sawrey and sister to Katherine and inherited Greenhead. He had a son William 1541-1607 who rebuilt Colton Church and left a will as of Greenhead and possibly another son Thomas.

William 1541-1607 married Margaret daughter of William Pennington of Colton. They had various children: John of the Ridding, William, Francis who was not the Vicar of South Kelsey in Lincolnshire, that Francis left a will mentioning numerous relations who do not relate to this family at all, Adam who was a fishmonger in London marrying in 1622 at St Matthew Friday St, Ellen Wheeler daughter of William Wheeler goldsmith. Adam died in 1630 and mentions relations in Furness in his will. He also has a number of apprentices. John Sands from the Fylde in Lancashire and presumably kin to the Rawlinson's Furness neighbours the Sands of Bouth. Another apprentice was James son of Francis Corker of Ulverston.

James's brother William became a fellow at Brasenose College, Oxford. Perceval Boyd produced a set of Inhabitants of London, which gives households. I don't know where he got his information from but in setting out Adam the fishmonger's family of wife and three daughters he adds a Francis Rawlinson as a visitor. There is a Francis Rawlinson citizen of London, amourer and brazier. One of his apprentices is Thomas Chamley son of William Chamley yeoman of Ashlack sworn to apprenticeship in 1623. Ashlack is in Furness.

Further children of William and Margaret were Robert said to be of Colton, Alice, Mary and Margaret. William who made his will 1619 at Greenhead bought land there from Christopher Sandes of Bouth, Anthony Sawrey of Plumpton and Thomas Rawlinson of Grizedale. K James VI & I sold off many manors and

Sandes, Sawrey and Rawlinson of Grisedale were probably acting for their neighbours.. William married in 1610 Margaret daughter of Walter Curwen of Mireside Cartmel . Their children included Robert who inherited Greenhead and Mireside and owned Cark Hall who features below, William who lived at Bucknall Hall Oxfordshire an army captain and Elizabeth who married first John Swainson of Cartmell Fell and secondly George Hutton of Thorpinsty

Early Rawlinson of Greenhead

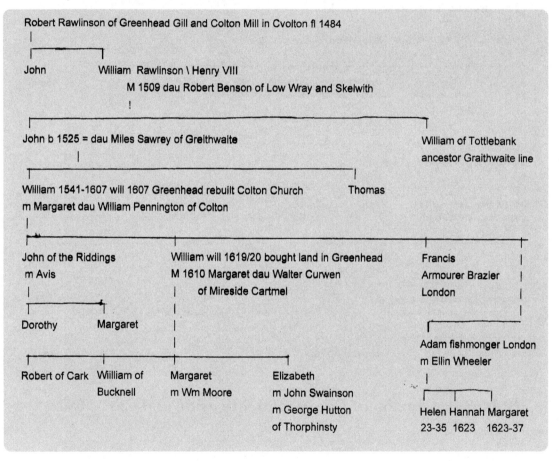

I propose to take them in the following order Cark, Angerton, Grizedale and finally Tottlebank, Graythwaite.

RAWLINSON OF CARK

Pedigree of Rawlinson of Cark

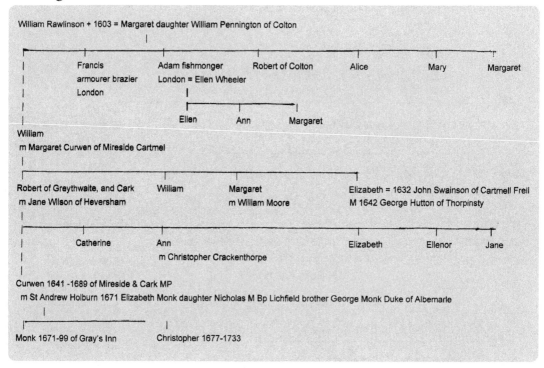

William Rawlinson + 1603 = Margaret daughter William Pennington of Colton

| | Francis armourer brazier London | Adam fishmonger London = Ellen Wheeler | Robert of Colton | Alice | Mary | Margaret |

Ellen   Ann   Margaret

William
m Margaret Curwen of Mireside Cartmel

| Robert of Greythwaite, and Cark m Jane Wilson of Heversham | William | Margaret m William Moore | Elizabeth = 1632 John Swainson of Cartmell Frell M 1642 George Hutton of Thorpinsty |

| Catherine | Ann m Christopher Crackenthorpe | Elizabeth | Ellenor | Jane |

Curwen 1641 -1689 of Mireside & Cark MP
m St Andrew Holburn 1671 Elizabeth Monk daughter Nicholas M Bp Lichfield brother George Monk Duke of Albemarle

Monk 1671-99 of Gray's Inn   Christopher 1677-1733

Robert Rawlinson of Greenhead, Mireside and Cark Hall 1610-1665

Robert was the elder son of William Rawlinson of Greenhead by his wife Margaret daughter of Walter Curwen of Mireside in Cartmel. William was in turn the son of William Rawlinson by his wife Margaret Pennington. Robert's father William during the reign of James VI & I commuted the customary or land rents by purchasing them from the crown,. The bloomery rents remained. Robert was a barrister educated at Gray's Inn . The family claimed he had suffered for his allegiance to King Charles I but he was never compounded and in 1647 he was

Cark Hall

appointed a Presbyterian elder of the ninth classis. Presbyterian churches come together in groups for various purposes. The classis corresponds to a deanery in the Church of England. In 1661 he became recorder of Lancaster. He probably conformed in 1662 when he was appointed vice chamberlain of Chester. In 1639 he married Jane daughter of Thomas Wilson of Heversham Hall. They had the following children :- Curwen 1641, Elizabeth 1643, Ann 1645, William 1647 (later of Bucknell Oxfordshire), Catherine 1654, Ellen 1656, Dorothy 1660 and Jane 1662.

He was a JP. The Wilsons of Heversham Hall also acquired Dallam Towers and became better known as Wilson of Dallam Towers

Curwen Rawlinson of Cark Hall 1641-1689

Curwen was the elder son of Robert Rawlinson by his wife Jane Wilson. He inherited Cark Hall and Mireside from his grandmother's family. He was baptised at Cartmel. He went to Queen's College Oxford. In 1672 at St Andrew Holborn he married Elizabeth daughter of Nicholas Monk Bishop of Hereford and brother of George Monk Duke of Albemarle who organized the restoration of King Charles II. He was steward of the Manor of Cartmel in 1660, a JP for Lancashire 1670-88, deputy lieutenant 1673-87 and captain of militia 1680-April 1688. He was reappointed to both these last posts in October 1688 and held them till his death. He was criticized for his partiality on the bench and was saved from dismissal by the Albemarle influence. He sat as a moderate Tory MP from January to August 1689.

He and his wife had two sons Monk 1671-92 and Christopher 1677-1733.

It was Curwen Rawlinson who produced the pedigree of his descent from Rawlinson of Greenhead. He also produced a pedigree of the Sandys family at the age of 16. Doubts have been expressed if a boy of that age could have produced such a document. However giving his station in life and his education it seems entirely possible granting his family gave him access to such material as they had

Christopher Rawlinson 1677-1733

Christopher was the second son of Curwen Rawlinson of Cark Hall by his wife Elizabeth Monk. He was born in Essex. He went to Queen's College Oxford in May 1695 but in June of the same year he moved to Magdalen College Cambridge. He was an antiquarian and in 1698 published an edition of King Alfred's translation of Boethius' "Consolation of Philosophy".

His mother's cousin was Christopher 2nd Duke of Albemarle and under his will Christopher Rawlinson was due to inherit the Albemarle estates providing he survived the duke's widow. However having been called to London because her grace was in her last illness he contracted small pox and died a month before her grace. He died at his lodgings in Holborn Row Lincoln's Inn Fields and was buried at St Albans. He had no children.

His will proved at Canterbury makes elaborate provision for his burial and monument either at St Albans or the Urswick Chapel in St Georges Chapel Windsor. His only sibling died before him without children. He had cousins through his father's sisters but he left all his land property to Richard Rawlinson the antiquarian q.v. for life. Richard belongs to a quite different branch of the family. A further example of the acknowledged cousinhood between Graythwaite and Grizedale

RAWLINSON OF BROUGHTON TOWER, ANGERTON and MARSH GRANGE

Rawlinson of Angerton, Broughton Tower, Marsh Grange, Sandscale etc

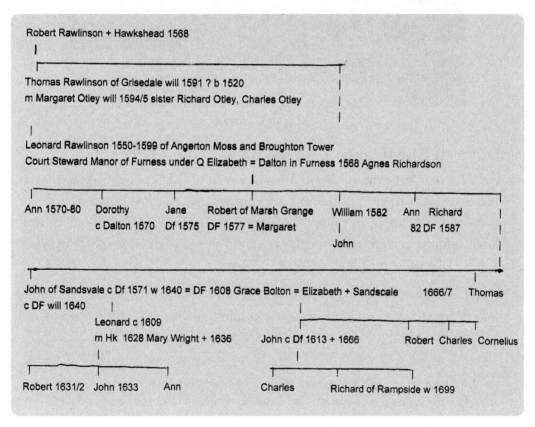

Robert Rawlinson + Hawkshead 1568

Thomas Rawlinson of Grisedale will 1591 ? b 1520
m Margaret Otley will 1594/5 sister Richard Otley, Charles Otley

Leonard Rawlinson 1550-1599 of Angerton Moss and Broughton Tower
Court Steward Manor of Furness under Q Elizabeth = Dalton in Furness 1568 Agnes Richardson

Ann 1570-80	Dorothy	Jane	Robert of Marsh Grange	William 1582	Ann	Richard
	c Dalton 1570	Df 1575	DF 1577 = Margaret		82 DF 1587	
				John		

John of Sandsvale c Df 1571 w 1640 = DF 1608 Grace Bolton = Elizabeth + Sandscale   1666/7   Thomas
c DF will 1640

Leonard c 1609
m Hk 1628 Mary Wright + 1636

John c Df 1613 + 1666   Robert Charles Cornelius

| Robert 1631/2 | John 1633 | Ann | | Charles | Richard of Rampside w 1699 |

Marsh Grange

Leonard Rawlinson of Angerton who died 1599

I take Leonard to be the brother of Thomas Rawlinson of Grizedale who mentions him in his will of 1591 or Thomas's son Leonard. Anyway this Leonard seems to have been born 1550, was steward of Low Furness under Queen Elizabeth and commissioned to survey Borrowdale in Cumbria for mineral working. He married Agnes Richardson at Dalton in 1568.

On 11 August 1582 a son of Leonard Rallinson's (sic) of Furnace (sic) Fells was drowned at Grange. Leonard and Agnes's children all baptised at Dalton were Ann 1569/0-80, Dorothy 1570, John 1571, Thomas 1574, Jane 1575, Robert 1577, Margaret 1579 William & Ann 1582. Leonard appears in the subsidy Rolls for 1581 and 1598. Of Leonard's children: John lived at Sandscale and he was in the subsidy roll of 1629 and Robert at Marsh Grange, he was in the subsidy roll for 1641. In the events described below John's widow is called Elizabeth and she is Royalist whereas the younger Leonard is a Parliamentarian. Dalton Registers give a wedding for John in 1608 with Grace Bolton, The younger Leonard is baptized 1609 son of John. John's other children all baptized at Dalton are John 1613, Robert 1615, Elizabeth 1615/6, Charles 1617, Cornelius 1619, Isabel 1622 and Mary 1625. I suspect the second marriage to Elizabeth would come before Charles or possibly between 1609 and 1613 which is the longest break in the children.

Leonard and his grandson Captain Leonard are the first individuals to be noticed. The documents tell of their attempts to acquire Marsh Grange, a property on the Duddon Coast of Low Furness, north of the modern village of Askam in Furness and South of Kirby in Furness. Sandscale is further South along the Duddon, Elliscales is a mile or two inland from Sandscale just north of Dalton. Angerton is two miles north of Marsh Grange and Broughton Tower three miles north of Angerton.

In 1580 Leonard Rawlinson purchased a moiety of Marsh Grange from William Askew, husbandman, whose mother Janet Askew was living at the property. In 1581 he bought the other moiety from William Askew. An apparently straightforward pair of transactions transferring the property from Askew to Rawlinson. However Askew had a brother Roger who claimed that William was not in a position to sell the second moiety as by rights it belonged to him. It came to court in 1586. Roger's claim was that his father, Richard Askew of Marsh Grange in his will of 1551 had left Marsh Grange to his wife Janet for ten years providing she did not remarry and after ten years to his two elder sons William and John, that John had died childless and as the sole remaining son of Richard he was entitled to John's share. Leonard Rawlinson's claim was that before Richard Askew had any claim to Marsh Grange it had been held by John Richardson and Richard Chambers by tenant right and they had conveyed it to William and that according to the custom of the manor, tenant right property could not be left by will to anyone other than the eldest son and therefore it was William's to sell. However when Roger dies in 1593 he is described as of Marsh Grange. Leonard died in 1599 at Angerton having married Agnes Richardson and they reputedly had six sons :-John 1571, Thomas 1574, Robert 1577, William 1582, Richard 1587 and Sawrey.

I am relying on Foster's pedigree for the existence of Sawrey Rawlinson. I can find no other evidence. Leonard left a will made in 1591 proved in 1599 making his wife Agnes executor and mentioning sons John, Robert, William & Thomas and a daughter Jane married to John Barbon and a nephew Robert Rawlinson. Leonard was a member of the twentyfour (effective rulers of Dalton in Furness) in 1579. In 1587 he was bailiff of the Royal Manor of Furness (Plain Furness). Along with James Anderton steward of the manor (and presumably owner of Bardsea) he was commissioned on the authority of the Queen to go to Borrowdale in Cumberland and discover who was a tenant in occupation of land belonging to the Manor of Furness. They found John Birkett, son of Nicholas Birkett, who had been a tenant under Henry VIII. who refused to pay more than one gold penny and William Braithwaite who refused to pay more than one year's rent. In the previous reign of Philip and Mary investigations had been made in Borrowdale into mineral resources.

John Rawlinson of Sandscale 1571-1640

John Rawlinson b 1571 married at Dalton in Furness in 1608 Grace Bolton and at a later date a lady called Elizabeth, (possibly a Gurnell from Millom,) and had several children including at least three sons of which the eldest was called Leonard and two others John and Robert. John died in 1640, when of Sandscale leaving a will now badly damaged making his wife Elizabeth executor and his brother Robert one of the supervisors. In 1631 he compounded £10 for refusing a knighthood.

Robert Rawlinson of Marsh Grange 1577-1649

Robert Rawlinson b 1577 was of Marsh Grange. So evidently his father Leonard did well out of the legal challenge. He was a papist and a recusant. On 27th September 1630, (6th year of Charles I) two parts of a capital messuage and 34 acres of land were seized into the King's hands. On 21st August 1634 he compounded with King Charles's Commissioners to pay a rent of £8 per annum for a lease of the same two parts and 34 acres. He is described as of Marsh Grange so presumably he was living there. He made a will in 1649 as of Marsh Grange and died the same year. He was at some stage fighting for the King against parliament. He took out a mortgage on Marsh Grange from John Preston of the Manor Esquire (the Manor House adjacent to Furness Abbey) for £100. Notwithstanding not having paid this off he offered to sell Marsh Grange to either of two nephews, Leonard son of John or William son of the third brother. Leonard refused on the grounds he was entitled to the estate anyway, but William accepted. However when they went to the Manor Court to ratify the deal. The steward of the court refused to do so on the grounds that Leonard was the rightful heir and that Robert was under sequestration..

Robert in his will leaves his estate at Soutergate to Roger and Ralph Kirkby, sons of his deceased brother in law, Anthony Kirkby of Gargrand (sic). He leaves an estate at Ireleth in Furness to John Kirkby, son of another deceased brother in law Roger Kirkby and to John's son Henry. He also makes this John Kirkby his executor. He leaves to John Kirkby and Leonard Rawlinson an estate at Scathwaite, granted to him by Thomas Fell together with all the estate of his late wife Jane. His executor is to obtain from his sister in law, Elizabeth Rawlinson of Sandscale, (widow of his brother John) as much of the money as John owed him as will pay off the mortgage to John Preston and to pay £199 Manorial dues. The children of his cousin William Rawlinson of Graythwaite are beneficiaries as are cousins Alexander and Cornelius Rawlinson and John and Robert sons of his brother John. When he died he left a widow Margaret who subsequently married his executor. She cannot be the Margaret who was sister to Anthony and Roger. John Kirkby the executor and later husband of Margaret cannot be the descendant of Roger Kirkby, father of Anthony and Roger, as that would have him marrying an aunt. So he must be a more distant relation. However both Margaret and Robert Rawlinson are described as cousins in Roger Kirkby of Kirkby's will of 1619

Captain Leonard Rawlinson of Sandscale, Marsh Grange and Scathwaite

The next member of this branch of the family was Captain Leonard Rawlinson of Sandscale. He was the eldest son of John Rawlinson of Sandscale and his wife Grace Bolton. He was in the subsidy roll for Dalton in 1641. His father died in 1640. He was the obvious heir to Marsh Grange as the eldest son of the eldest brother of Robert and heir to Sandscale as eldest son of John. In addition by his uncle's will he had a part share in Scathwite, a hamlet North of Ulverston, in Egton cum Newland. In December 1643 or January 1644 he joined the parliamentary army under Colonel John Moore. An affidavit of Colonel Moore's dated 22 July 1645 stated that Rawlinson had been in his regiment a year and seven months. Moore also stated that Rawlinson had a wife and children. Moore tells us Rawlinson served at Liverpool and was taken prisoner by Prince Rupert's forces and held prisoner for a long time and that during his time away from his estates he was plundered of all his estates. Since his release Rawlinson had raised another company and was still helping in the defense of Liverpool and was at the date of the affidavit in London on public employment of himself (Rawlinson and other officers of his regiment)

Captain Rawlinson's problems started with the fact that as far as his family were concerned he supported the wrong side. Not only was his Uncle Robert a royalist but so was his mother (probably step mother) and two younger brothers. Rawlinson was in captivity fourteen weeks during which time he was plundered of

11

£200 and had no allowance from the state for his imprisonment. Sir John Mainey who was in Furness at this time stopped all Leonard Rawlinson's rents. His mother having at this time two sons, John and Robert and her servants in arms against Parliament took advantage of her son Leonard's imprisonment. With a warrant from Sir John Mainey she took possession of diverse parcels of the said Leonard's estate claiming that her late husband had given her a lease of the same and only now was she able to take advantage of it. She already had a moiety for life. Also there is the sale to Leonard's cousin William Rawlinson which was disallowed by the steward of the manor. However it seems the said steward, who had an estate adjoining Marsh Grange, had a desire to acquire Marsh Grange thinking that Leonard's financial condition would force him to sell. When he saw that the Committee in Goldsmith's Hall was minded to allow Leonard to compound and that Captain Leonard Rawlinson was not ready to sell he changed his tactics and tried to buy William Rawlinson's interest for £500 and worked at making good the deed made under sequestration which had been rejected in open court.

William Rawlinson may be the same as Captain William Rawlinson who petitioned on behalf of his infant son John and stated that after sequestration Robert Rawlinson had conformed to the Church of England. There was a Captain William Rawlinson in Colonel John Moore's regiment and a William Rawlinson from the Tottlebank side of the family was a captain of militia for the parliamentary side during the civil war. We shall have more to say about him later.

Leonard however had compounded and paid in his moiety and obtained an order from the Committee of Goldsmith's Hall for possession. This order was intercepted at the post house by an adverse party; the farmers of Sir John Preston's estate, on behalf of Mr John Pym's children, seized Marsh Grange on the basis of the £100 mortgage owed by Robert Rawlinson to Sir John Preston . These people then leased Marsh Grange to the steward's father in law who is called a father of one of the farmers. The steward of the manor asked Captain Leonard Rawlinson to put the matter to arbitration saying he would help him and his cousin William come to an agreement. The steward said William would give Leonard £200 if Leonard would bind himself to enter into arbitration and that further the steward who was counselor to Leonard's mother would bring to an end the suite between Leonard and his mother which had been running seven years. If Leonard refused so good an offer it would cost him as much in suite before he got it. Captain Leonard Rawlinson refused the offer. He went up to London and paid to the

Committee of Haberdashers Hall £100 due to Sir John Preston and by order of the said committee took possession of his estate. The steward bragged that he would overthrow this by various pretenses, which was to seize the premises on behalf of Mr Pym's children for the £100 mortgage not withstanding that this had already been paid by Leonard Rawlinson.

Captain Rawlinson made a series of petitions to the national authorities. In one, received 15 June 1649, he said he had compounded for a messuage at Scathwaite worth £10 which messuage had been kept out of his possession and therefore had derived no benefit from his composition and so asked for an abatement of the cost of the composition. He asked them to bear in mind that he had served his faithful service since the beginning of these troubles, that he had been plundered three times by the King's party and last summer by the Scots under the late Marquis of Hamilton.

On 18th January 1649, presumably 1649/50, he petitioned for relief for the £100 composition he had paid for Marsh Grange stating he had had no benefit from the composition as the land had been detained from him and one William Rawlinson pretending a deed from Robert Rawlinson then a papist in arms is trying to compound for the estate.

On 15 February 1649/50 Rawlinson is again stating that he is kept out of Marsh Grange and Scathwaite and asking that the Governor of Lancaster Castle, Captain Rippon be directed to put him into these tenements.

On March 29 1649 (This is probably 1649/50 even though the year ended March 25th) the Committee for the Advance of Public Money reciting that Robert Rawlinson of Marsh Grange deceased had in life owed John Preston of the Manor Esquire a recusant and delinquent £100, that the petitioner had paid the £100 in satisfaction of the debt owing to John Preston and the committee had accepted it in satisfaction: ordered that the petitioner stand harmless against said John Preston and all others touching the debt and further ordered Thomas Jervis and Thomas Hammersley officers of the committee to repair to Marsh Grange, enter and take possession and deliver premises over to Leonard Rawlinson and in case of resistance to break down doors and locks and all colonels and captains to be aiding and assisting of the same.

This matter is illuminated by an exchange of letters between Captain Leonard Rawlinson and Colonel John Moore, evidently a member of the Committee for Advance of Money:-

Starting 9th June 1648 a statement that Robert Rawlinson delinquent late of Marsh Grange had mortgaged Marsh Grange to John Preston delinquent for £100; that Leonard Rawlinson his nephew and heir had compounded for it, will pay the £100 and desire to be secured against Preston and put in possession of the mortgaged land.

On the same day a deposition of Leonard Rawlinson relative to the mortgage and a debt of £150 due by the late John Rawlinson of Somerscale (presumably Sandscale) whose executrix is Elizabeth his widow. The bonds for both debts are in the hands of Margaret widow of Robert Rawlinson now married to John Kirby Robert Rawlinson's executor.

21st June 1648 Order by the Committee that Elizabeth Rawlinson is to pay in the £150 and Kirby is to deliver up the bonds.

The next letter from Leonard Rawlinson is on 16th September 1648 living at Broughton Tower to Colonel John Moore of Charring (sic) Cross He refers to the miseries the Furness area had sustained since the arrival of the Scots. He had fled when the Cavaliers entered the area and at his mother's instigation his house was plundered his horse taken and he and a servant were accused of treason for pursuing Lord Digby and Sir Marmaduke Langdale's men when they passed through the country. Meanwhile she had entertained the cavaliers at dinner all the time they stayed in the country and suffered not a penny loss. He asks Colonel Moore to forward his petition to the House for his uncle's estate. He has served an order on his mother as he had written previously, but does not think she will appear to show cause. He finishes by saying he lives near a mother who plots his destruction: - for no one else's house in Furness has been so badly treated and further she has seized his meadow which deprives him of subsistence.

He writes to Colonel Moore again on 28th September. He has delivered the order to his mother, but she slights it.. He asks Colonel Moore to do what is needful and order Kirby and his Aunt Margaret to send the bonds at once. He asks for details of the sums due to Abrathat Tench so he can pay him. Otherwise he is reluctant to enter any corporation in Lancashire for fear of a writ. He advises Moore to get stewardship of the Manor of Muchland for Moore's nephew Alex Rigby, as it had been in Rigby's family for time out of mind.

On **11th January 1649** (new style) There is a deposition of Richard Tomlinson minister of Dalton in proof of the debt of £150 borrowed from Robert Rawlinson by John Rawlinson who offered to the widow Elizabeth to forgive the debt if she would be content to be at peace with her son Leonard. She replied with great passion that she would never have it forgiven on such terms. She also asked Tomlinson to burn the bonds that Leonard had left in his custody but he refused.

8th February 1649 Order by Committee for securing of Elizabeth Rawlinson's estate, for non-payment of £150 owed by John Rawlinson to Robert Rawlinson

9th February Order by Committee to two officers of County Lancaster to seize, inventory and secure the rents, goods and estate of Elizabeth Rawlinson for non-payment of said £150 with writ of Assistance

Letter from Leonard Rawlinson to Colonel John Moore 13th February sent from Preston:

> *My cousin Hunter has not farmed Marsh Grange, but Fell has devised a new scheme to keep me out of it. Mr Pym's children have an ordinance for certain sums out of (John) Preston's estate and the trustees have given a lease to that old knave John Askew on account of a debt of £100 borrowed of old Mr Preston on that security and my uncle's house was searched and all his writings taken.*

According to the printed Committee Minutes the next bit is part of Leonard Rawlinson's letter

> *I discovered the £100 for your use and you ought to have it as the discoverer, as it is redeemable on payment, as it was not Preston's money but his lands that were granted to Pym's children. They challenge also £120 which Tomlinson discovered of Preston's money, and which you ought to have as you discovered it before. Jarvis should be sent down to seize for your use Marsh Grange and Nicholas Gardiner's estate, and my mother's estate for the £150, Captain Ripon, Governor of Lancaster Castle, should help him with troops and a warrant should be sent to deliver up Rob. Rawlinson's writings. Porter and Thompson, the trustees, will clear £700 this year, "thus go the public moneys away to such prowling knaves," but I believe*

on a word from you Pym would order them not to meddle with the Marsh Grange lease. Fell who aims at it, was not one of those who helped in this great work, "but lurks in the country to see the event of things, that he may come in smoothly when the coast is clear," and Askew, his father in law, has been in arms against Parliament. Pray discover his estate, and I will find you proofs to sequester him.

Ask Captain Ripon to send me soldiers for Kirby's lease is out on 12th February and I want to enter into possession before Askew can take it. Pray help me to place of receiver for the monthly taxations, etc for Ireland.

[29 March 1649] Petition to Committee for Advancement of Moneys by Leonard Rawlinson Captain under Sir John Moore. Compounded for Marsh Grange, County Lancaster as heir to his uncle Robert Rawlinson, a delinquent. The tenement was mortgaged to Sir John Preston, delinquent whose estates were given by Parliament for the use of Mr Pym's children under trustees. John Askew, father of one of the trustees (presumably father in law) entered forcibly the tenement as belonging to Sir John Preston's estate and sowed part of the land. The petitioner having paid off the mortgage by an order from your committee, re-entered the premises and sowed the rest of the land, but now Askew comes forcibly to reap the corn from the whole of the land. He begs an order to Askew to pay for the corn sown by the petitioner and to Colonel [Thomas] Birch, Governor of Liverpool to maintain him in possession of the premises

29th March 1649 Order by Committee for Advancement of Moneys that Leonard Rawlinson who has compounded for the estate of his uncle, a delinquent and paid £100 debt owing to Sir John Preston, be indemnified therefore, and that the committee's officers repair to Marsh Grange, take possession, break open locks if needful, and deliver it to Leonard Rawlinson.

18th May 1649 Order by Committee that Kirby be brought up in custody to show cause why he has not as ordered brought in 2 bonds of £100 and £50 between Robert and Elizabeth Rawlinson

1st August 1649 Order by Committee to Treasurer Lane to pay to Colonel John Moore £100 received from Leonard Rawlinson, in part of arrears due to him for Parliament service

3rd August Petition of John Askew of Elliscales, County Lancaster to be established in possession of the premises, at least for a year, having been at expense in fencing and sowing seed, but Leonard Ra\wlinson came on their warrant 29th March., with some troops, broke open the doors, and turned him out . He is willing to pay to Rawlinson the rent contracted for

3rd August 1649 Order by Committee that the present tenant, not having had time to get in his crops, be permitted to occupy till 25th March next.

12th September Order by Committee for Advance of Money that on Leonard Rawlinson paying to the tenant of Marsh Grange the costs of ploughing, sowing, manuring, etc, he be allowed to enjoy the crop and retain the premises.

2nd November 1649 Order by Committee that as the tenant refuses to surrender the premises Colonel Birch Governor of Liverpool enforce the former order and put Rawlinson in possession

As John Askew only had two daughters and one of them Margaret was married to Judge Thomas Fell., it would seem clear that Judge Fell was the steward of the manor who wanted possession of Marsh Grange for himself and used his position as a trustee for the Pym children as a means to that end.

Marsh Grange is a mystery. John Askew is attested their in 1634 but by 1649 is of Elliscales. Roger Askew of Marsh Grange leaves a will in 1593 and Richard Askew of Marsh Grange, who may be Roger's son. makes his will in 1657. George Fell of Marsh Grange makes his will in 1670 and hands Marsh Grange over to trustees on behalf of his daughter who sell it to Thomas Lower married to a sister of George Fell and daughter of Judge Fell. It looks as though Judge Fell in the end succeeded in his manoeuvres

Sir John Mainey Bt came from Linton in Kent. The spelling of the name varies;- Mayney, Mayne, Mainey, Meiny. He had been made a baronet by Charles I in 1631. At the outbreak of the Civil War he rallied to the king with a troop of horse and was sent North with Newcastle's forces. In March 1644 he was the messenger taking Newcastle's appeal to Prince Rupert then at Liverpool, asking for Rupert's assistance. As well as the letter he was charged with a verbal report. He fought at Marston Moor (April 1644) which was a defeat for the royalists who then retreated into York. Horse regiments were not a lot of use in sustaining a seige and Newcastle sent his cavalry subsequently known as the Northern Horse away. However Mainey collected a brigade consisting of the remains of five regiments (his own, Sir William Pelham's, Sir John Preston's, Sir Robert Dallison's and Sir William Eure's) and came to Furness partly to recruit extra soldiers and partly to collect rents due to the king.

Mainey's quarters were at Dalton. He had his horse in a field near Sir John Preston's house. There were ships belonging to parliamentary forces lying near Pile of Fouldry. The parliamentarians attacked having taken into a little town said to be "not two musket shots away from our horse" (presumably either Hawcoat or Newton in Furness) which had a pinfold in the middle of it. The royalists won; those parliamentarians in the pinfold were either captured or killed. 200 foot soldiers were captured and sent to the king, 17 sailors and some wealthy locals were captured and ransomed. The royalists chased the parliamentarians to the sides of the ships.

Mainey attacked North Scale on Walney then held by the parliamentarians. The first attack failed. On the second attempt the village was deserted and the parliamentarian ships had sailed. Every house in North Scale was demolished except two known to belong to royalists. He succeeded in collecting the money. Plain Furness was a royal manor and the rent from all the tenants came to £500 a year. Three years were owing and he collected the full £1500. He also collected £500 in ransoms from the prisoners. He assembled the tenants at Ulverston and enlisted them in royal service but only to defend Furness. They were not willing to serve outside Furness. He was entertained by Sir John Preston in Cartmel, presumably at Holker, till they were pressed by Colonel George Dodding on one side and the Scots on the other. Later on he attempted to relieve Carlisle but failing that seized a 1000 head of cattle. Later he did a forced march to relieve Pontefract, delivering the cattle in part to the royalist garrison at Skipton and the rest to Pontefract. He was later sent south with a message for the king. At one stage he was badly wounded and died a poor man.,

In March 1644 he carried a letter from Newcastle to Prince Rupert requesting his assistance in Yorkshire.

Of the younger Leonard's brothers / half brothers and sisters John 1613-66 had the following children all baptised at Dalton ; - Charles 1647/8, Margaret 1651/2, Elizabeth 1652, Richard 1653, Hester 1656, William 1659, Mary 1665. of these only Richard is of any note. He is described variously as of Dalton and Rampside, There is an extant letter from him describing himself as servant of Thomas Richardson of Roanhead,.He features with Thomas Richardson in the 1691 Tripartite Indenture by which Daniel Abraham bought out all other interests in Swarthmoor Hall and for some reason Swarthmoor passed through the hands of Rawlinson and Richardson.. In 1684 he married Mary Knipe of Hawkshead. In 1699 he left a will leaving everything to Mary and hypothetical children and grandchildren. His widow married Thomas Richardson at Aldingham in 1711.

RAWLINSON OF GRIZEDALE
HAWKSHEAD AND LONDON

Thomas Rawlinson of Grizedale died in 1613

He was a son of Robert Rawlinson of Grisedale who mentions a son Thomas in his will of 1606 himself the son of Thomas and Margaret Rawlinson of Grisedale. Thomas's (the father) will was dated 1591. Margaret Rawlinson also left a will, Her maiden name was Otley.

In 1608 at Hawkshead Thomas married Susanna Steinberger als Stonehewer. She is said to have been born in Keswick, 1597 daughter of Mark Steinberger by his wife Anna Maria Hochstetter daughter of Daniel Hochstetter of Keswick and Derwent Isle by his wife Radegunda Stamlet. Daniel Hochstetter, born at Augsburg in Germany was the leader of the German Miners of the Mines Royal based in Keswick and working the surrounding fells. Thomas and Susanna had the following children all baptized at Hawkshead Thomas 1609+ 1654 (apprenticed to his brother Daniel ante 1650), Robert 1612, Daniel 1616, Elizabeth, Radegunda and Susanna who married George Browne of Troutbeck in 1623. This George Browne built Townend House now belonging to the National Trust. Beatrix Potter bought the house from the last of the Brownes

Dugdale in his visitation pedigree of 1663 identifies Thomas son of John of Greenhead not with Thomas of Grisedale but with the Thomas who married Esther daughter of Adam Sandys and widow of John Sawrey. However the likelihood is that that Thomas is the son of William of Tottlebank which fits better with the Sawrey pedigree. William of Tottlebank and later Graythwaite was the first to take an interest in Force Forge and his son Thomas followed on leaving Force Smithy to his daughter Hester (by Esther Sandys).

Daniel Rawlinson of the Mitre Fenchurch St

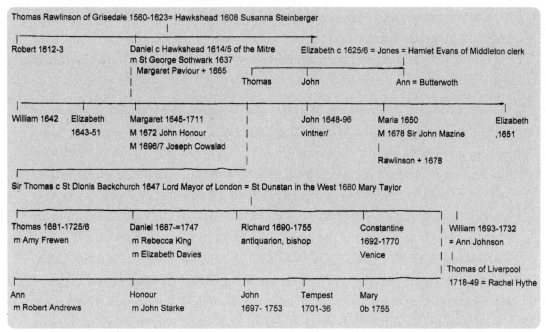

Thomas Rawlinson of Grisedale 1560-1623= Hawkshead 1608 Susanna Steinberger

Robert 1612-3	Daniel c Hawkshead 1614/5 of the Mitre m St George Sothwark 1637 Margaret Paviour + 1665		Elizabeth c 1625/6 = Jones = Hamlet Evans of Middleton clerk
		Thomas John	Ann = Butterwoth

| William 1642 | Elizabeth
1643-51 | Margaret 1645-1711
M 1672 John Honour
M 1896/7 Joseph Cowslad | John 1648-96
vintner/ | Maria 1650
M 1678 Sir John Mazine

Rawlinson + 1678 | Elizabeth
,1651 |

Sir Thomas c St Dionis Backchurch 1647 Lord Mayor of London = St Dunstan in the West 1680 Mary Taylor

Thomas 1681-1725/6 m Amy Frewen	Daniel 1687-=1747 m Rebecca King m Elizabeth Davies	Richard 1690-1755 antiquarion, bishop	Constantine 1692-1770 Venice	William 1693-1732 = Ann Johnson Thomas of Liverpool 1718-49 = Rachel Hythe
Ann m Robert Andrews	Honour m John Starke	John 1697- 1753	Tempest Mary 1701-36 0b 1755	

Daniel Rawlinson of Hawkshead and London 1616-1679

Daniel was third son of Thomas Rawlinson of Hawkshead and his wife Susanna Steinberger. He was apprenticed 5/2/1632/3 to Ellen Spillman of the Vintners Company London. He was free in 1639. On 3/12/1639 his brother Thomas was apprenticed to him. In 1644 he had his nephew, Thomas Evans, vintner, and Mary his wife living with him. In 1645 he administered the will of John Richardson citizen & tanner of All Hallows London Wall who apart from £5 for his mother and six shillings to buy Daniel's son William a bible left the whole of his estate to Daniel. A list of his apprentices is appended in the following excursus. Among them are Daniel's son Thomas, Robert son of Daniel's deceased brother Robert, brother Robert' s other son Daniel was apprenticed to John Billingshey. This Daniel became Master of the Vintner's Company in 1739. He married Billingshey's daughter Elizabeth, John Billingshey had also been Master of the vintner's company in 1679. Returning to Daniel's apprentices Thomas Evans is probably the Thomas Evans vintner living with Daniel. Daniel was Master of the Vintners Co in 1678. He was in partnership with his son Thomas Daniel kept the Mitre Tavern in (1657), Fenchurch St. Mitre Court is almost opposite the site of The Mitre. A letter of his grandson Richard Rawlinson the antiquary to Thomas Herne non juring antiquary of Oxford states "Daniel Rawlinson who kept the

Mitre Tavern in Fenchurch St of whose being suspected in the Rump Time I have learnt much, the Whigs tell that up on the king's murder 30th January 1649, he hung his sign in mourning". This naturally put him out of favour with the Cromwellians, however his hospitality to churchmen was such that he throve again and got a good estate.

Daniel paid for the rebuilding of Hawkshead School in 1675 and in the same year he supported the rebuilding of the chapel of ease at Satterthwaite. He was a wealthy man at his death; he owned land in Wasperton Warwickshire, Waltham Cross in Essex, Saddlebare in Norfolk as well as land in Grisedale which he had bought from his brother Robert. He was a friend of Samuel Pepys, who enjoyed his venison patties, and features in his diary. On one occasion he made it possible for Pepys to view from a balcony the burning of two acts of parliament by the public executioner at the Exchange. One was the act setting up the Commonwealth. On another he took Pepys to a Jewish service. In 1662 he entertained Pepys to supper where they discussed a disturbance in a church in Friday St in which some young people had interrupted the service by shouting "Porridge". Pepys reports the death of Daniel's wife, Margaret of the plague in 1665 together with that of a maid servant and a manservant all in Fenchurch St.

His business was burnt down in the great fire of London. He subsequently rebuilt the Mitre. He had the walls painted by Isaac Fuller. Horace Walpole gives a description "Isaac Fuller was much employed to paint the taverns particularly the Mitre in Fenchurch St. over the chimneys there were a Venus, a Satyr, a sleeping child, a boy riding a goat, another fallen off, Saturn devouring a child, Mercury, Minerva, Dianna, Apollo, Bacchus, Venus and Ceres embracing a fallen Silenus fallen down and holding a goblet into which a boy was pouring wine. The scenes between the windows showed the seasons and on the ceiling in a large circle two angels supporting a mitre".

Very little of Fullers work survives as it was on walls which have subsequently been demolished. However, there is an extant portrait by Fuller of John Bradshaw who presided at the trial of King Charles I.

Daniel married Margaret Paviour at St George the Martyr Southwark in 1637. They had surviving four children Thomas, John, Margaret wife of John Honour and Maria wife of Sir John Mazine. Sir John Mazine, a courtier evidently sought an introduction because of the dowry that Daniel was offering. He used his acquaintance with "a respected relation to get permission to court Mary Rawlinson". The phrase respected relation comes from a book on the English Middle Class. However a Chancery Case between Sir Thomas Rawlinson and Sir John Mazine shows that the person referred to was called William Rawlinson who lived in the district called Poultney and had a father in law called James Moseley. The question is "Was this William Rawlinson a relation at all?". There was a William Rawlinson who settled at Bucknell in Oxfordshire but he died in 1643 and there was Sir William Rawlinson the MP for Hendon. Both these Williams belong to the Greenhead, Graythwaite branch. We know two wives of the MP and neither was called Moseley. However this William Rawlinson does donate a book to Hawkshead School Library. Further he has a book plate inserted in the book he donated saying his father was born at Greenhead and was called William. This opens up the possibility that William Rawlinson of Bucknell could be the father of William Rawlinson of Poultney in which case he was a relation from the Graythwaite branch.

Both William Rawlinson and his father in law James Moseley were in favour of the match and believed that Mazine was a good deal richer than actually turned out. There were disputes between Thomas Rawlinson, Daniel's son and Maria's brother and Sir John Mazine about the marriage settlement and land at Carberton in 1680 Mazine was the son of the John Mazine of Carberton Notts, who served under the Marquis of Newcastle in the Civil War. He left a will in 1705. The marriage was at St Dionis Backchurch in 1678 The only known child a son, Rawlinson Mazine, was buried at St Dionis in 1678. The other daughter Margaret married firstly John Honour and after his death Joseph Cowslad of Donnington in Shaw near Newbury.

It is said that Daniel's portrait hangs in Hawkshead School having been moved there when a London Church was demolished in 1838. The portrait in Hawkshead Museum formerly the school is an etcthing by George Vertue of Daniel's son Thomas. Daniel made a bequest to Hawkshead School in 1672 Hawkshead Museum is said

Hawkshead Museum

to have been built by Daniel after the fire, plague and wife's death. Many of the books he donated are there. He paid Hearth Tax in 1662 in St Olave Hart St.

Towards the end of his life in June 1678 Titus Oates launched the Popish Plot alleging " a general rising of catholics, a massacre of protestants, the burning of London, the assassination of the king and the invasion of Ireland by a French army" To begin with he was successful and 35 catholics were executed including five Jesuits and Viscount Stafford. Daniel Rawlinson wrote a letter to Sir Daniel Fleming of Rydal 16/2/1677 regarding the disappearance of William Fleming and taxation. This William is possibly Sir Daniel's eldest son who was later made a baronet. There is a further letter on 19th-23rd February 1677/8 regarding taxation and William Fleming. On 28th December 1678 Daniel Rawlinson writes to Daniel Fleming "the men condemned were to have been executed today but the King is said made somewhat scruple in respect of the truth of the testimony of Oates and Bedloe and they were reprieved. But now the evidence of the silversmith has brought full credence to their story" The silver smith was Miles Prance whose evidence lead to the execution of three innocent artisans. He did recant but not until much later

Daniel was apprenticed to Ellen Spillman 1632/3. Who she was is a bit of a mystery. One possible clue is that shortly before 1631 Edward Organ was appointed beadle. In 1631 he petitioned the Vintner's Court for financial assistance he had children and had become a livery man. The court did help him and his children but in 1633 he died and further assistance for the children was paid to a Mr Spillman who had married the children's aunt. Spillman is not a particularly common name. .

I have managed to find out a liitle about Edward Organ, First an earlier Edward Organ was buried at St Dunstan Stepney in 1603 while living at the Swan in Ratcliffe. Next Edward Organam attains freedom with the vintners in 1607. As Edward Organ he had three apprentice vintners William Troughton, in 1612, John Read in 1617 and Gabriel Bazill in 1620/1. He married Margaret Haring at St Mary Whitechapel 1614 who was buried in 1623. They had the following children Mary in 1617, Ellen in 1619 who was buried 1628, Thomasine 1619, Thomas 1620, Nicholas 1621 and Alice in 1623 All these children were Baptised at St Dionis Backchurch and wife Margaret and daughter Ellen were buried there. There are two funeral references for Edward Organ one at St James Garlickhythe described as on of the Vintners on 6 9 1632 and shortly afterwards Bedlam as a pauper. These might be the same man first the funeral then the internment.

None of this amounts to proof that Ellen Spilman had any connection with Edward Organ but the closeness of the dates and use of St Dionis both by Organ and Rawlinson and the absence of any other reference to Mr Spilman make it worth including this information in case further information might elucidate the matter.

Excursus 1
Daniel Rawlinson's apprentices

All the below were apprenticed to a Daniel Rawlinson vintner of which there were several

1/ Daniel Rawlinson 1616-1679 of the Mitre

2/ Daniel Rawlinson 1654-1701 son of the above's elder brother Robert

3/ Daniel Rawlinson 1676-1701 son of the immediately above's elder brother Robert. This one was subsequently apprenticed to the East India Company and died on board ship en route to Batavia

4/ Daniel Rawlinson 1678-1747 son of No 2 Master of the vintner 1739

Thomas Rawlinson his brother

Robert Brethwaite son of William Brethwaite of Sawrey 2 4 1650

Robert Turner son Henry Turner of Ambleside 6 5 1652

John Dykes son of Robert Dykes of Petlow, Hodnet Shropshire 2 11 1654

William Knipe son of William Knipe yeoman Grisedale 2 1 1654/5

William Chamley son of William Chamley yeoman of Bethecar 6 4 1658

John Forty son of George Forty yeoman Wotton Underwood Buckinghamshire 5 2 1660/1 of

Thomas Evans son Hamlet Evans clerk Middleton Lancashire 3 9 1661

Thomas Rawlinson his own son 16 9 1663

William Athey son of John Atchey citizen and haberdasher 2 2 1663/4

Nathaniel Pertesoyle son of Thomas Pertesoyle yeoman Shoenestead Huntindon-shire 6/11/1664

Thomas Wenhouse son of William Wenhouse yeoman of Cartmell 2/2/1663/4

Thomas Painter son of John Painter citizen amd haberdasher 4/7/1665

Benjamin Turner son of Henry Turner citizen and broderer 6/11/1666

Robert Ingle son of Edward Ingle yeoman Paddington 11/4/1666

Robert Rawlinson son of Robert Rawlinson of Grisedale Satterthwaite gentleman deceased 8/11/1667

Peter Lowe son of Edward Lowe mercer Middlewich Cheshire 1/9/1668

George Wood son of George Wood gentleman Whitehaven 3/11/1668

William Pratt son of Thomas Pratt citizen and barber surgeon 2/2/1668/9

Lufton Turode son of Charles Turode gent North Ockenden Essex 6/4/1669

John Pierrepont son of Ralph Pierrepont gent Leominster Herefordshire 4/5/1669 turned over to Thomas Brett

Thomas Glover son of Thomas Glover gentleman London deceased 2/5/1671

Daniel Rawlinson son of Robert Rawlinson gentleman Grizedale Satterthwaite deceased was apprenticed to John Billingshay 24/12/1673

William Roger son of William Roger yeoman Satterthwaite 4/7/1682

Hugh Adderley son of Hugh Adderley deceased 5/2/1682/3

Simon Liversage son of Michael Liversage doctor of medecine of Leicester 9/10/1684

John Postlethwaite son of Thomas Postlethwaite of Satterthwaite shoemaker 7/4/1685- This man became a vintner in Limehouse and his son was Malachy Postlethwaite 1707-1767 an early writer on economics prior to Adam Smith. He advised Robert Walpole for many years. and afterwards worked for the Africa Company (set up to provide African slaves for the Americas) producing an enthu-siastic economic defence of the company.

John Folard son of John Folard citizen ironmonger 7/12/1687

William Ivory son of William Ivory citizen and upholder 4/4/1688

Walter Holte son of Thomas Holte gentleman of Staines Mddx 3/10/1688

Daniel Rawlinson son of Robert to his father 25/5/1691 (27/11/1694) turned over to Thomas Carver

William Potter son of Thomas Potter mercer of Harbury Warwickshire 5/7/1692

Edwin Sandys son of Thomas Sandys upholder of East Whelthall Lancashire 4/10/1693

John White son of John White gentleman of Holton Oxfordshire 20/6/1696

Thomas Ames son of Thomas Ames citizen and haberdasher 6/6/1699

John Holles son of Thomas Holles gentleman Newcastle upon Tyne 4/3/1700/1

Thomas Potter son Thomas Potter innholder of Bicester 3/11/1702

Thomas Rawlinson son of Clement Rawlinson of Hadfield Broad Oak Essex tallowchandler to Daniel Rawlinson vintner 2/2/1708/9

Excursus 2

There were a number of Daniel Rawlinsons. Some of them contemporary with each other. All engaged as vintners, distillers, wine cooper or the like. Starting with Thomas Rawlinson of Grisedale who married Susanna Stonehewer at Hawkshead in 1608. They had among others Richard born 1612/3 and Daniel 1616-79 who was the lessee of the Mitre and fried of Pepys. Richard 1612/3 had among others, two sons Daniel 1654-1701 who was at St Mary Newington Butts and died at Crutched Friers and Robert. Daniel 1654-1701 had land in St Mary Newington including Kent St and left a widow Elizabeth who died at Reigate and among others two sons Daniel and Robert. This third Daniel married at Reigate in 1726 Deborah Jones who in turn died at Battersea leaving land at St Mary Newington Butts and Kent St which had come from her late husband. The third Robert became Rector of Charlwood Surrey. He had two son called Daniel (possibly died young), one called Robert and the second Sir Thomas Lord Mayor of London. Reverting to the second Robert he had a son Daniel 1676 or 1673 who died on the Ruby in 1701 on route to the East Indies and a son Thomas. Turning to the first Daniel, he of the Mitre. One of his sons was the first Sir Thomas, Lord Mayor of London and he had among others a son Daniel who died young and another also called

Daniel baptized at St James Garlick Hythe in 1687 who married Rebecca King in 1702, divorced her in 1709 for adultery after the death of their only known child in 1703 and remarried in 1740 Elizabeth Davies. They were both of St Olave Hart St. Daniel died in 1747, a merchant wine cooper of Crutched Friers and Master of the vintners in 1739. Elizabeth was involved in law suits about Crutched Friers when Daniel's widow

Excursus 3
Books donated to Hawkshead Grammar School Library by Daniel Rawlinson vintner of The Mitre Fenchurch St and associates

Daniel Rawlinson

Kindred
Curwen Rawlinson of Cark MP

John Honour of Hadley Middlesex son in law

Mrs Elizabeth Howkins of Hadley, mother of above by an earlier marriage

Mr John Howkins of Hadley, stepfather of John Honour

Sir Thomas Rawlinson son Master of Vintners, Lord Mayor London

William Rawlinson cousin St Mary Walnoth Poultney

Mrs Mary Rawlinson daughter

Robert Rawlinson nephew distiller London

John Blashfield citizen and fishmonger in law of preceding

John Rawlinson linen draper London son

John Sharpe DD Archdeacon Berkshire brother in law Sir William Rawlinson cousin

Sir John Mazine equerry to the king son in law

Daniel Rawlinson son of Daniel Rawlinson the Mitre great nephew

Hawkshead locals and ex students HGS
John Sands of Foulyeate

James Bowness – master HGS 1669-1671

John Sandys born Graythwaite brazier, forger citizen London

George Wilson of Fieldhead

Christopher Edmundson minister of Hawkshead

Allen Wilson citizen Vintner London son of Mrs Elizabeth Nicholson born Hawkshead Hall

Christopher Nicholson merchant Newcastle son of deceased Christopher Nicholson also merchant Newcastle but born Hawkshead Hall.

Richard Hutton rector of Bootle Cumberland

George Wilson gentleman of Blackhall Kendal

Myles Sandys of Graythwaite

Henry Nicholson minister of Colton

John Sadler schoolmaster Hawkshead

Edmund Garforth vicar Lancaster

Thomas Preston Snr Holker in Cartmel

Daniel Fleming of Rydal

Francis Medcalfe of Lancaster

George Rigge parish clerk Hawkshead

William Wells vicar Millom

John Christopherson usher Hawkshead Free School

John Kirkby gentleman Coniston Hall

Vintners

Elizabeth Benson wife Thomas Benson late master Vintner's Co

John Kent vintner St Olave Hart St

Edward Ainge gentleman Clerk to the Vintner's Co

Samuel Hall late warden Vintner's Co

Sir William Wale late Alderman City of London, late Master Vintner's Co, former employer

HM Ordnance Office

Major Nathaniel Brookes- The Angel Cornhill bookseller and stationer HM Ordinance Office

Sir Jonas Moore- mathematician, surveyor general HM Ordinance Office

Edward Sherburn translator HM Ordinance

George Wharton treasurer paymaster HM Ordinance

Others

William Gibbon treasurer Christ Church Hospital London

John Wilson gentleman

John Chomley gentleman

Thomas Archer of Warwickshire

Benjamin Baron of Westcott Gloucestershire

John Flavill of Birchen Lane London – kept coffee house near Fechurch St

Thomas Martyn gentleman of his Majesty's privy chamber in ordinary

Joseph Thompson rector St Dunstan in the West

John Tillison receiver general and clerk of works rebuilding of St Paul's

John Viner citizen distiller at the Hermitage near Wapping

John Hardy of Bonehill near Finsbury

Lawrence Stanyon son of Abraham Stanyon

Daniel Mills rector St Olave Hart St

Edward Browne fellow Clare Hall Cambridge

George Crawley chirurgeon, Billiter Lane London

Moses Pitt bookseller The White Hart, Little Brittain

Dr George May rector St Dionis Backchurch

John Linger plumber Leadenhall St

Dr Sancroft   Dean of St Paul's later Archbishop of Canterbury

Edward Clayton of Waltham Abbey Essex

Richard Beckford esquire late Alderman City of London

Charles Johnson

James Pilkington rector Croston Lancs

John Pearson   Bishop of Chester

Dr Edward Layfield – Archdeacon Essex , Canon St Paul's

Robert Carr of Gray's Inn

Richard Brooke of Lambeth

John Smith author & Rector St Mary's Colchester

William Allington

Thomas Wilson citizen and draper Lime St

John Daniel gentleman Lincoln's Inn

John Bagnall gentleman Staffordshire

Hyet Edmundson rector Market Deeping Lincolnshire

Simon Corbett yeoman rider to the king

Sir Thomas Rawlinson 1647-1708 Lord Mayor of London

Thomas was the son of Daniel Rawlinson 1616-79. He was born in the parish of St Dionis Backchurch and baptised in 1647, He joined the Vintners Company in 1670 and was master in 1687 and 1696. He was a friend of Sir Thomas Kinsey, who had married his wife's aunt Mary Hill.

Sir Thomas Rawlinson

Kinsey was Sheriff of London 1685-6. He and Rawlinson did what they could to keep James VII and II on the throne, spending £10,000 between them in this cause according to Thomas Hearnes account of Richard Rawlinson one of Sir Thomas's sons. He intended to stand for parliament in 1685 against Roger Kirkby to the latter's indignation. He was President of Brideswell and Bethlehem Hospitals in 1705.

There is an etching by George Vertue, said to be after a portrait by Sir Godfry Kneller, in the National Portrait Gallery. There are copies of this etching in Hawkshead Museum and the Rawlinson papers now in Bodley's Library, Oxford. The whereabouts of the painting by Kneller is according to the Kneller Catalogue in the Bridewell Hospital Collection. King Edward School Witley and associated junior school are the Bridewell Foundation. The portrait of Rawlinson by Kneller hangs in the senior school. This makes sense as Sir Thomas was governor of the Bridewell and Bedlam Hospitals. The Vintner's do have a painting of Sir Thomas but not by Kneller. They also have a sword rest belonging to him with his arms. He was Master of the Vintners in 1687. Sir Thomas was Lord Mayor of London 1705.

While he was mayor Marlbrough won his victories in Flanders and at his request the Queen granted the trophies from Ramilies to be hung in the Guildhall. He made a will in 1700 with a codicil in 1707 Hawkshead School was a beneficiary. His portrait by Vertue is in the Guildhall. He had land in Grisedale, Essex, Surrey and Wasperton in Warwickshire. He married Mary Taylor eldest daughter of Richard Taylor of Turnham Green who kept the Devil Tavern by the Temple. He may have been Master of The Vintner's Co 1677. . She died 1725 having married twice more to Stephen Hutchinson and Michael Lister. Stephen Hutchinson in his will left everything to Dame Mary Her financial settlements and separations from her third husband were a financial embarrassment to the family. Michael Lister was of Burwell Lincolnshire. Quite what his relationship to the main line of that family is I cannot say. Their children were Thomas 1681-1725, Daniel 1687, Richard 1690-1755 William 1693, John 1696, Constantine 1698, Tempest 1701, Mary, Ann 1694.and Honour 1695 and a number of children who died young. He left £12000 in stock of the East India Company. He invested in the first Tontine in 1696 in the names of his sons Daniel and Thomas and that of his wife Mary.

He is easily the most prominent member of the St Dionis congregation. Many of his children are buried at St Dionis, though baptized at St Sepulchre Holborn. Thomas's father seems to have made a fortune. I suspect Thomas lived up to his income. None of his children seems to have had any great urge to make money preferring to live on their asets and in some cases beyond their assets. Thomas, William and John all got into financial difficulties, Daniel became a distiller. Despite what it says on the Memorial to Sir Thomas formerly in St Dionis he wasn't the one who died in 1701 on the way to the East Indies. A Daniel Rawlinson who died on the way to the East Indies repeatedly referred to his father as Robert Rawlinson and Robert Rawlinson proved the will. Thomas and William invested in the South Sea Company and were ruined by it. Mary had at her death in 1763/5 £2600 stock in something called Old South Sea Annuities.

Honour married in 1732 John Starke who had plantation property in Virginia, had served in India where he married his first wife Martha Empson who was the mother of his three children Richard, John and Martha. Honour had no children and she was buried at Ewell, John may be the John Starke widower of Mitcham who married at Ewell, Elizabeth. His last wife was Anne Clutterbuck. His mother's will in 1725 was witnessed by Honour's sister Mary who was a great friend of John's daughter Martha and indeed shared a house, 12 Upper Cheyne Walk, with her from 1748-59

Honour died in 1751 and was buried at Ewell. She had attended in 1750 a sermon preached before Charles Duke of Richmond and Lennox in aid of the London Hospitals. Also attending was her cousin Sir Thomas Rawlinson the second Lord Mayor of London of that name.

The other daughter to reach adulthood Ann married Robert Andrews a dry salter to whom for a while Tempest Rawlinson was apprenticed. They had two daughters Honour and Ann. They are mentioned in Mary's will. At some stage Tempest presented his niece Honour Andrews with a copy of London Cries. Tempest also helped his brother Richard with the sale of Thomas's books

William, as mentioned, earlier, got into debt and moved to Antwerp where he married Amy Johnson and according to Enright's pedigree of these Rawlinsons had several children including Thomas of Liverpool (see below)

John was an officer in the First of Foot but also got into debt and was exiled by Richard to Cheshire. He died at Little Leigh

Constantine accompanied his brother Richard on his second continental tour. He settled in Venice where he was visited by Walter Rawlinson son of the second Lord Mayor.

Sir Thomas had a map made of his Grizedale Estate in 1696 presumably with an attempt to sell Grizedale. There is a copy in the Rawlinson Papers in the Bodleian and printed in "Whats in a name" a book of maps of Rusland Valley showing field names by Rusland Horizons Trust. The house is shown on the estate map diagram fashion showing each room.

Joseph Foster in his pedigrees of Lancashire families credits Thomas with another son Clement but gives no information about him. I can find no referene to either a baptism or burial of Clement nor does he appear in any of the wills that mention his brothers and sisters. I assume he doesn't and didn';t exist and was a mistake of Fosters and not the only one either. There was a tallow chandler, called Clement Rawlinson, at Hadfield Broadoak Essex and his younger son was apprenticed in 1708/9 to Daniel Rawlinson vintner (this would be no 4)

Thomas Rawlinson 1681-1725

Thomas was the eldest son of Sir Thomas Rawlinson Lord Mayor of London by Mary

his wife. He was born at the Old Bailey in St Sepulchre parish, educated at Eton and St John's College, Oxford and the Middle Temple. He was called to the bar in 1705. On his father's death 1708 he inherited a fortune. He was a great collector of books, housing so many at his residence in Grey's Inn that he was obliged to sleep in a corridor. He acquired London House, Aldersgate to house his books. He may be the model for Joseph Addison's "Tom Folio - a learned idiot".He was a governor of Bridewell and Bethlehem Hospitals in 1706, a governor of St Bartholemew's in 1712, a Fellow of the Royal Society in 1713 and a member of the Society of Antiquaries in 1724. In 1724 he married his servant Amy Frewin formerly a maid in a coffee house in Aldersgate St. They had no children. He died in 1725.and was buried at St Botolph, Aldersgate He was financially ruined by his investment in the South Sea Bubble. The South Sea Company was established to pay off the national debt by selling African slaves to the American plantations. His book collection was sold off in various lots between 1622 and 1634. His widow married John Tabor in 1725 at St Paul's Cathedral

Richard Rawlinson antiquary 1690-1755

Richard Rawlinson[1]

Richard was the third son of Sir Thomas Rawlinson Lord Mayor of London. He was educated at St Paul's School, Eton College and St John's College Oxford. In 1688 when James VII and II was exiled and replaced by William III and Mary II a number of Anglican Bishops including the then Archbishop of Canterbury refused to take an oath of allegiance to King William. They were known as non jurors. Richard war a supporter of the Stuart Kings and was ordained into the Non Juror Church, eventually being consecrated a bishop and in time senior bishop. He was a bibliophile and antiquarian. He purchased a lot of his brother Thomas's books on orientalia in 1734. When his brother died in 1725 having left all his money to his widow who remarried, Richard who had been administering the family estates for his brother bought his widowed sister in law out for an annuity. He still had to deal with his brother's insolvency so continued to sell off his brother's books, assisted by his brother Tempest. His brother Constantine settled for an annuity and went to live in Venice. His brother John had left the army and then went bankrupt. Richard settled him in Cheshire on £10 a year.

1: Photo by permission of the President and Fellows of St John's College, Oxford

William, his eldest remaining brother had moved to Rotterdam as a trader but had been ruined in the South Sea Bubble and died in 1732 leaving a widow and a 14 year son called Thomas. Richard was a friend of the antiquarian Thomas Hearne and wrote a life of Anthony Wood. Later in life he fell out with both the Royal Society and the Society of Antiquaries, cutting the latter out of his will. He began transferring his collection to the Bodleian Library Oxford. 1750 almanacs ranging in date from 1607 to 1747, arrived between 1752 and 1755. After his death a collection of over 5000 manuscripts went to the Bodleian.

On 11th August 1750 he gave money to found the Professorship of Anglo Saxon at Oxford and partly financed it with income from the rectories of Ulverston and Pennington, along with various properties in Low Furness, including, Roose Mill, Little Mill and Walney Water Mill which he had purchased from Thomas Lower and his wife Mary, daughter of Judge Fell of Swarthmoor, together with Orgrave Mill, vacaries at Greenscoe, Greenhaume, Thwaite Flat, Mill Flat and Crake Mill. He died in 1755 at his home London House, St Botolph,. Islington. His heart is in a memorial at St John's College Oxford who also benefited from his will. He left a sum of money to be divided between his brother Constantine of Venice, his sister Mary Rawlinson, his sister Ann Andrews and Rachel widow of his nephew, Thomas Rawlinson. He left property in Fulham to Hertford College and other property in Fulham to the Society of Antiquaries. He also left his brother John property in Devonshire Rd, London.

Windmill at Walney

Roose Mill

Little Mill in Dalton

He wrote books of history and antiquities of various places including Salisbury Cathedral, Bath Abbey, Rochester Cathedral, Glastonbury and the memorials at Canterbury Cathedral.

Despite his brothers' involvement in the South Sea Bubble and his nephew's attempt to break into the slave trade Richard himself was opposed to slavery and among the restrictions on who could hold the professorship he had established were plantation owners, along with members of the Royal Society, married men, Scots and Irish.,

Rawlinson Rd in Oxford is named after him. The land would have belonged to St John's College when the road was laid out.

In 1718 he made an extensive tour of Oxfordshire looking at epitaphs and collecting bits of historical information. He was sometimes accompanied by his brother, Thomas and his brother John also helped having just completed his degree at Corpus Christie. He also had further assistance from his brother Tempest. Brian Enright who wrote a D Phil Thesis on Richard Rawlinson quotes two references to his nephew Thomas's death. One, which I have seen the original refers to his shock at his nephews decease, the other says "Such is the fate of those who engage in this wicked and unnatural commerce". Unfortunately Enright's reference is wrong and I haven't found the correct one. This is interesting in view of his brother's willingness to invest in the South Sea Company. He refers to his nephew,s death as taking place off the Guinea Coast and his niece in law talks of the Gulf of Babone which is also off the coast of Africa, while the letter to the Evening News implies Thomas survived till they got to Antigua.

Excursus 4

The Deed of Trust and Will of Richard Rawlinson of St John the Baptist College Oxford published at the appointment of the testator

11/8/1750

Bargain & Sale

1/ Richard Rawlinson St

2/ John Markham apothecary Paternoster Row; John Locker of St Helen London esquire & Edward Umfraville of the Inner Temple

For 5/- in money and various considerations

All that annual fee farm rent of £43 of the rectory of Ulverston granted by letters patent of King James I, 17th February 6 James to John Fleming esquire and John Ambrose gentleman + fee farm rent of Ulverston Glebe of 12/- occupied by Leonard Hutchinson + fee farm rent of two mills under one roof on the Crake known as Crake Mills granted by letters patent 11th February 7James 1 to Edward Ferrars mercer & Francis Phelips gentleman + fee farm rent of £6 from rectory and church of Pennington granted by letters patent 8th May 7James 1 to Francis Morris and Francis Phelips + vacary or hardwick known as Greenham in Dalton in Furness and 10 acres at Greentern granted by letters patent 25th September 4Charles I to Edward Ditchfield, Humphrey Clark & Francis Mosse + fee farm rent of Sandscale with Rushby Close, Oker Sandscale Cow Close, Inchfield Close in Sandmarsh by letters patent of 4 Charles I as above+ fee farm rent of vacary or hardwick at Whateflet and Greensike by letters patent of 4th year of King Charles I as above + fee farm rent of Sheepcoat called Stainyard by letters patent 9th January 21JamesI to Edward Badby and William Wallden + fee farm rent of three mills Rouse Mill, Little Mill and Orgrave Mill by letters patent 9th May 7James I to Edward Ferrars and James Phelips all sold in 1676 by indenture by Sir Robert Carr Kt, Bt and Sir William Ellis Kt to Daniel Rawlinson And fee farm rent of £2/7/8 with Greenscoe Wood, New Close Baystone Bank by letters patent of 25th September 4 Charles I to Edward Ditchfield, John Highland, Humphrey Clark Francis Mosse and sold to Daniel Rawlinson by indenture 12th September 1676 by said Sir Robert Carr and said Sir William Ellis to the use of the said Richard Rawlinson for life then as directed in his will. In his will he directed that this property be used to establish a Professorship of Anglo Saxon at Oxford.

Thomas Rawlinson of Liverpool 1718-1749

Thomas was the only son of William Rawlinson, one of the sons of Sir Thomas Rawlinson, Lord Mayor and nephew of Richard Rawlinson. Richard apprenticed Thomas to a shipbuilder in Liverpool. As the last male Rawlinson Thomas was his uncle's obvious heir. Richard hoped that Thomas would in time both assist and contribute to running the families estate However Thomas did not agree and after making what his uncle considered an imprudent marriage he agreed to surrender all claim on the estate in return for 1000gns to buy and equip a ship which was done and called "Snow". In 1748 the ship left Liverpool with Thomas as captain and sailed with dry goods for Africa, they arrived at Bonane in Cameroon. They sold the dry goods and took on board 120 slaves who were fastened in irons and battened down below hatches. Fifteen of them soon died of sickness. On 5th June 1749 while riding at anchor near Antigua the slaves rebelled killing most of the crew and running the ship aground and escaping taking with them all the goods and property including the crew's clothing. Captain Rawlinson had previously left the ship with three armed canoes hoping to suppress the rebellion but died soon after. The mate, Thomas Clerk, wrote a letter 6th September 1649, explaining all this which was published in the London Evening Post December14[th]-16th. Rawlinson had married Rachel Hythe at Sefton in 1738; they had six known children, Richard born and died 1740, Catherine born and died 1741,Amy baptized St Peter Liverpool 1743 and married at St Nicholas 1766 to John Williams a joiner, Honour baptized St Peter 1744. Dorothy baptized same 1745 married at St Nicholas 1763 James Barkley smith of Tarleton St, Liverpool and Ellen baptized St Peter 1748. Thomas is referred to as merchant. Honour married (signing with a mark) Robert Kewley a cooper of Liverpool. They had 11 children of whom 8 died as small children one as a teenager and the other two girls as spinsters. Dorothy and James Barkley had two sons Rawlinson and William, both died as babies. Rachel remarried at Ashton under Lyne in 1755 to Richard Colshed an attorney at law. As Thomas was an only nephew of Richard Rawlinson it looks as though there is no main line descendant of Daniel Rawlinson of the Mitre.

In appendix 3 is an account by the mate of Thomas's ship of their disasterous voyage, copied from the **Daily News**. Actually one of the Rawlinson papers is a full page of the **Daily News** containing this item

Robert Rawlinson of Grisedale, Charlwood

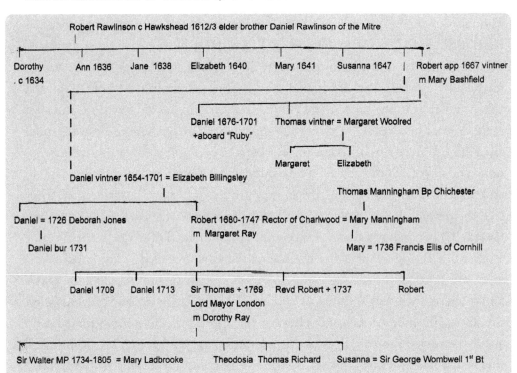

Robert Rawlinson distiller

Was the son of Robert Rawlinson yeoman baptised Hawkshead 1612, an elder brother of Daniel Rawlinson vintner of the Mitre who died before 1667.

He was apprenticed to his uncle Daniel in 1667.

He had the following apprentices;

4/12/1674 his brother William, son of Robert Rawlinson, yeoman Grisedale deceased

9/4/1678 James Penny son of James Penny, yeoman, Grisedale

17/8/1685 Robert Banister son of Robert Banister, gentleman, Essex

25/5/1691 his own son Robert who in 27 11 1694 was turned over to Thomas Carver.

His son Thomas was apprenticed 6 12 1693 to John Brown vintner

Robert Rawlinson Rector of Charlwood

Robert's father, Daniel, was a son of Robert Rawlinson, second son of Thomas Rawlinson of Grisedale and elder brother of Daniel Rawlinson, vintner, of the Mitre, Fenchurch St. His father Daniel was apprenticed as a vintner to John Billingsley in 1673. John was Master of The Vintners 1679. Robert's mother was called Elizabeth (probably Billingsley the daughter of John Billingsley). She was born 1653 and died at Reigate in 1721. Robert was baptised at St Dionis Backchurch in 1680. He was educated at Trinity College Cambridge and was Rector of Charlwood from 1711-47. His father Daniel Rawlinson had bought the right to make the next presentation to the Rectory of Charlwood, from Sir William Throgmorton. Robert's father Daniel Rawlinson was jn dispute with the Revd Henry Hesketh, then, Rector of Charlwood who also claimed the right. Evidently this was resolved in Rawlinson's favour. Both Daniel's were vintners, Robert was a prebendary of Chichester Cathedral and Chaplain to the Royal Regiment of Scots Guards. In 1716 a gallery for minstrels was added to the church. He was first married in 1705, at Denham to Margaret Ray in 1737 there was buried the Revd Robert Rawlinson junior who was a son who had been educated at Bury St Edmunds Grammar School and admitted to Trinity College Cambridge in 1723. . He had three other sons, Daniel who was baptised at Charlwood in 1713, Thomas who became Lord Mayor of London in 1753 and Richard. After his first wife's death he married Mary Manningham, daughter of Thomas Manningham Bishop of Chichester by whom he had a son Manningham and a daughter Mary who married Francis Ellis.

He was buried at St Dionis Backchurch in 1747 in the same year as his father who was then a merchant of St Olave, Hart St.

Sir Thomas Rawlinson of Stowlangtoft + 1769

This Sir Thomas was also Lord Mayor of London. He held the office in 1753. He was the son of Revd Robert Rawlinson of Charlewood Surrey . He is in fact a cousin twice removed of the other Sir Thomas Rawlinson who was also Lord Mayor of London. There is a pedigree that identifies him with Thomas Rawlinson nephew of Richard Rawlinson the antiquary, but this is impossible as that Thomas died in 1749 off Antigua..

Thomas married his first cousin Dorothy daughter of Revd Richard Ray Rector of Haughley, at St James Garlickhythe in 1734 when he was of All Hallows, Steyning. They had seven children, Walter, Theodosia, Margaret, Thomas, Richard and Susanna who married Sir George Wombwell 1st Bt, governor of the East India Company. Richard Ray was vicar of Haughley from 1702-58 when he died. Thomas was a partner in the firm of Rawlinson and Davison, dealers in coffee, tea, sugar etc of Creechurch Lane in the City of London. The firm also had premises at the "Three Sugar Loaves" 45 Fenchurch St. Rawlinson's predecessor as owner of the firm was Walter Ray, who would be uncle both of Thomas and his wife Dorothy. Walter was apprenticed to Paul Garnier from 1699-1706 and was warden of the grocer's company in 1724. Thomas was apprenticed to Walter Ray in 1725, became a freeman of the grocer's company in 1734 and Master in 1747.

Stowlangtoft Hall in 1880

In Kent's Directory for 1736 Thomas Rawlinson is listed as grocer of Fenchurch St. In 1740 Rawlinson took as his partner Monkhouse Davison and they became Rawlinson and Davison. Monkhouse Davison. had become a freeman in 1738, he had witnessed Walter Ray's codicil in 1737. They were joined by Abram Newton a cousin of John Constable the painter, who married a sister of Davison's . After Thomas died the firm became Davison and Newton. It was their tea which was thrown into the harbour by the Boston tea party in 1773.

In 1758 Thomas leased two houses in Fenchurch St from the Earl of Dartmouth and, in 1762, he, Monkhouse Davison and Abram Newton bought the premises in Fenchuirch St from the Earl and Countess of Dartmouth. Thomas purchased Stowlangtoft in 1760 and died at Fenchurch St in 1769 leaving a will. He was buried at Haughley. His wife had died in 1761 and was buried at Haughley.

It was in 1789 Davison and Newman bought 4/18 of the Rose Hall Estate in St Thomas in the Vale, Middlesex, Jamaica . It was a slave plantation growing sugar cane with over 200 slaves. This was 20 years after Rawlinson's death. Thomas and Dorothy did well out of Dorothy's connections, most importantly through their joint uncle Walter Ray. They also between them received legacies from Richard Ray vicar of Haughley, Dorothy's father, from Revd Francis Astry DD of Harlington, a pluralist, who was married to Dorothy's maternal aunt Susanna Walklate, from John Waldren of St Margaret's Westminster a cousin of Dorothy's mother Margaret Ray nee Walklate and Dame Elizabeth Sanderson of Ickleford Hertfordshire who described Dorothy's mother Margaret as a niece. Actually she was a cousin. She was the daughter of Samuel How of St Gregory's London by his wife Dorothy Walklate daughter of Gregory Walklate grocer and citizen of London and sister of Thomas Walklate who was Margaret's father.

She married twice; to William Degge (a cousin as her mother was a Degge) and to Sir William Sanderson. They also inherited from Mrs Dorthy How, Elizabeth Sanderson's mother and from Mrs Maria Clissold widow of Roger Clissold of London who claimed to be Dorothy's mother's aunt. She was the daughter of Jonathan Blackwell sometime Sherriff of Bristol who was responsible for laying out the passageway now known as Christmas Steps.

An excellent representation of a certain wise body with a hall in the East going to pay a visit to a certain great body in the West.

**Members of the Corporation who support the Peace of Paris and the presentation of their address at St James's Palace 12/5/1763.
Sir Thomas Rawlinson has a coffee canister and a sugar loaf on a pole.**

Sir Walter Rawlinson MP 1734-1805

Walter was the only son of Sir Thomas Rawlinson, who died 1769. He was educated at Bury St Edmund Grammar School and Trinity College Cambridge. He married Mary daughter of Sir Robert Ladbroke a banker. He went into partnership with his father in law as a banker. He was MP for various seats from 1774 to 1790. He was President of the Bridewell and Bethleham Hospitals He died in 1805 leaving no children.

RAWLINSON OF TOTTLEBANK AND GRAYTHWAITE

Rawlinson of Tottlebank, Graythwaite and Rusland

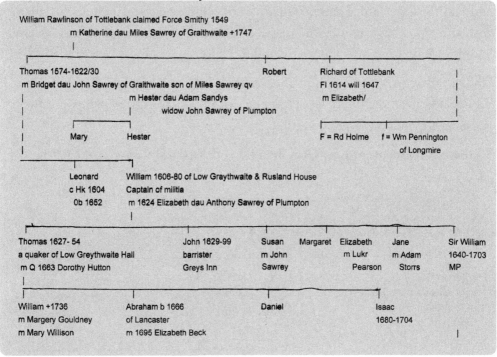

William Rawlinson of Tottlebank claimed Force Smithy 1549
m Katherine dau Miles Sawrey of Graithwaite +1747

Thomas 1574-1622/30
m Bridget dau John Sawrey of Graithwaite son of Miles Sawrey qv
    m Hester dau Adam Sandys
        widow John Sawrey of Plumpton

Robert

Richard of Tottlebank
Fl 1614 will 1647
m Elizabeth/

Mary   Hester

F = Rd Holme   f = Wm Pennington
                            of Longmire

Leonard   William 1606-80 of Low Graythwaite & Rusland House
c Hk 1604   Captain of militia
Ob 1652   m 1624 Elizabeth dau Anthony Sawrey of Plumpton

Thomas 1627- 54   John 1629-99   Susan   Margaret   Elizabeth   Jane   Sir William
a quaker of Low Greythwaite Hall   barrister   m John   m Lukr   m Adam   1640-1703
m Q 1663 Dorothy Hutton   Greys Inn   Sawrey   Pearson   Storrs   MP

William +1736   Abraham b 1666   Daniel   Isaac
m Margery Gouldney   of Lancaster   1680-1704
m Mary Willison   m 1695 Elizabeth Beck

RH Richard Rawlinson of Tottlebank

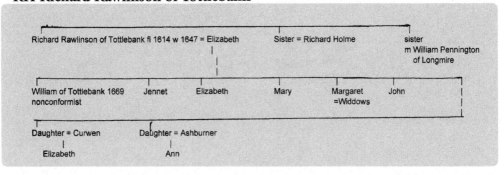

Richard Rawlinson of Tottlebank fl 1614 w 1647 = Elizabeth   Sister = Richard Holme   sister
                                                                                           m William Pennington
                                                                                               of Longmire

William of Tottlebank 1669   Jennet   Elizabeth   Mary   Margaret   John
nonconformist   =Widdows

Daughter = Curwen   Daughter = Ashburner
Elizabeth   Ann

William Rawlinson of Tottlebank

William's wife Katherine had previously been wife of John Sawrey. John Sawrey and William Sandys had been granted the right to cut enough timber to provide charcoal for three ironworks including Force Smithy. After John died it all went to William Sandys but William and Katherine went to court in 1549 claiming Katherine had a right as John's widow and obtained Force Smithy and a third share of another. This in due course passed down to William's son Thomas 1574-1639 who left it to his daughter Hester. Thomas moved from Tottlebank to Graythwaite, married Bridget/Jane Sawrey only daughter and heir of John Sawrey of Graythwaite and had sons Leonard, Henry, William 1608-80 see below, daughters Elizabeth and Ann. After his wife died he married Hester daughter of Adam Sandys and widow of John Sawrey of Plumpton and had further daughters Hester and Mary.

William had further sons Robert and Richard and two daughters. Richard was at Tottlebank when the house was registered for nonconformist worship and there is a chapel there now, Tottlebank Baptist Chapel

William Rawlinson of Low Graythwaite and Rusland Captain of Militia

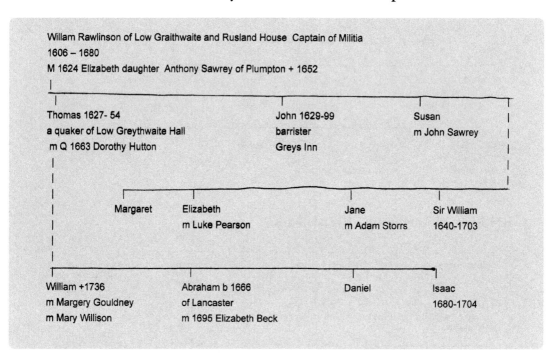

William Rawlinson of Low Graithwaite and Rusland House Captain of Militia
1606 – 1680
M 1624 Elizabeth daughter Anthony Sawrey of Plumpton + 1652

Thomas 1627- 54	John 1629-99	Susan
a quaker of Low Greythwaite Hall	barrister	m John Sawrey
m Q 1663 Dorothy Hutton	Greys Inn	

| | Margaret | Elizabeth | | Jane | Sir William |
| | | m Luke Pearson | | m Adam Storrs | 1640-1703 |

William +1736	Abraham b 1666	Daniel	Isaac
m Margery Gouldney	of Lancaster		1680-1704
m Mary Willison	m 1695 Elizabeth Beck		

Captain William Rawlinson, Captain of Militia. 1608-80

There were several people called Captain William Rawlinson. First was the nephew of Robert Rawlinson of Marsh Grange who if the son of Robert's third brother would be the son of Robert's brother William. He had an infant son John at the time of the dispute about Marsh Grange. I cannot say what side he was on in the Civil War.

Second in J M Gratton's list of parliamentary and royalist officers in Lancashire 1642 -1651 we find a Captain William Rawlinson in John Moore's regiment. He may be the same man as the first one.

Third we have William Rawlinson Captain of Militia who seems to have been answerable to Colonel George Dodding. He was the son of Thomas Rawlinson and his wife Bridget Sawrey and grandson of William Rawlinson of Tottlebank and his wife Katherine a daughter of Miles Sawrey of Graythwaite. His parents were cousins and he inherited Graythwaite. He was 22 in 1630. His father Thomas died in 1623 and had messuages at Graythwaite and Cunsey and another at Rusland. In 1624 William married Elizabeth daughter of Anthony Sawrey of Plumpton. He was High Constable of Furness and Cartmell in 1633. In 1643 he raised a troop of seventy horse and served with them till 1648. He fought at Marston Moor, Ribble Bridge and in Furness. He captured a Major Munday who had fought at the seige of Lathom. Munday was subsequently executed by parliamentary forces.

After the Civil War he opened up Force Forge helping to revive the iron industry. In 1655 there is a bond of £200 between him and Charles Crowe requiring Crowe to cease his ministry at Hawkshead and find a replacement. He died in 1680. His children were Thomas, John and Susan who married John Sawrey of Plumpton

In 1647 Captain Rawlinson was asked by George Dodding and Judge Thomas Fell of Swarthmoor; who was Lt Colonel of George Dodding's regiment, to raise money for parliament in Lonsdale Hundred. Later that year he was asked to appear at Ulverston to produce bills of assessment. In 1649 he was asked by the same two to return horse and troops to their proper townships so that they may be available for the safety of the country. In 1649 with Rowland Dawson and Richard Braithwaite he takes a lease on Cunsey Forge formerly made between William Wright of Brougham and Myles Sandys. 1n 1652 he was paying Hugh Forth, a farmer, excise duty on iron worked at Cunsey Forge

At some stage he bought Gilthwaitrigg and adjoining pastures etc from the Pickerings, Sleddalls and one Mitchel.

In his will of 1680 he leaves nothing to his eldest son Thomas who had become a Quaker and banned from his father's house. The estate was left to the second son John and his issue but if he had no such issue a corn mill and fulling mill at Force went to Thomas's second son, Abraham and failing that Thomas's eldest son William. It seems the actual succession after William was John, the second son, William (Sir William) third son and then William son of Thomas. William had married Elizabeth Sawrey who had survived him. They had the following daughters: Alice married to William Thornton of Hornby, Susan married to John Sawrey of Plumpton, Margaret married to Henry Bateman of Old Hutton, Jane married to Adam Storrs of Storrs, Elizabeth married to Luke Pearson of Gressingham and after his death to William Curwen of Helsington, Ann married to Richard Chatburn of Melling, Mary married to John Burrows, soap boiler of Derby, the mother of John Grigg and Francis Grigg, the mother of Miss Escrigg, wife of John Hudson of Haverbrack, Rebecca wife of James Towers of Kendal. Some of these daughters are known only from references to sister Curwen, sister Benson, sister Towers in family correspondence and certain wills. It is noteworthy that four of the girls moved to the Melling Hornby area on marriage which was where brother Abraham had a house.

Excursus 5
Papers relating to Captain William Rawlinson's activities.
BD/HJ/90/17 at Barrow Archives

A/

The account of Captain William Rawlinson, captain of a troop of Volunteers consisting of 70 horse, raised without being a charge to the state, about the 2nd of October 1643, being from henceforth kept in readiness for the service of the King and Parliament, only in actual service these times following :-

First/ When the Baronett Curwen with share of Cumberland force advanced upon Millom, being on the borders of this county of Lancaster. We were then commanded to Kirkby and lay there 4 days till they retreated.

Second/ About the 1ˢᵗ of January on Saturday we were commanded to Lancaster, when it was noticed that Sir James Gillington and Sir Wm Bradshaw being then in Yorkshire were on the march towards Lancaster with forces and stayed there till Wednesday

Third/ Three days attendance at Brathay Bridge a passage along the borders of Westmorland, when Sir Christopher Lowther with Cumberland forces marched that way to Kendal.

Fourth/ when we were commanded to Manchester upon the seventeenth of May 1644. Prince Rupert being taken into the county and retreated to Lancaster and the service to Yorkshire till the 29ᵗʰ of September following.

Fifth/ and there upon several alarms, as when Colonel Gray took Kendall, and upon several orders from Colonel Alexander Rigby and we went over sands, when report was oft forth coming to Chester to raise the siege, and several other alarms to the number of 22 days or thereabouts

Sixth/ when the Lord Digby marched towards Scotland and retreated back on service and conducting the prisoners to Lancaster Castle, that time 12 days

B/

73 horse and a half charged on Furness and Cartmel

Kirkby constable wick 4 horse

Dunndale & Scathwaite 3

Ulvston wholl townshipp 15

Penington 02

Aldingham township 05

Urswicke townshipp 04

Lecce townshipp 03

Dalton pish 09

Hauxhood constablrwicke 06

Colton constable wick 04 and a half

Broughton in Cartmel 07 and a half

Holker township 06

Alithwaite township 04 and a half

"Tho Fell"

[presumably this is Judge Fell a Lt Colonel in George Doddings Regt}

C/

These are to certify to all to it whom it may concern, that Captain William Rawlinson of Graythwaite in the County of Lancaster gentleman commanded a troop of horse for the service of parliament for the space of five years last past. And it was in the said service at Marston Moor a battle. And did very good service at Ribble Bridge in Lancaster and took Maw[e] Munday and his company in Furness. And hath done several other faithful and honest service for the parliament at all such time or times as he had any opportunities to advance the said service

Feb 14th 1648

Will Swift	Tho Fell
Adam Sandys	Tho Rippon
Nathaniel Nicholson	John Sawrey
Tho Wither	W West
Willm Gardn	Tho Hunter
James Thornton	Willm Wither
Tho Wigmore	James Bacchus

D/

You are appointed by the Commissioners in the ordinances of Parliament for raising the sixty thousand Pounds a moiety to be collected of the moneys to be raised by virtue of the said ordinance for six months within the hundred of Lonsdale, on this side of the sands, which moneys you are to have in your hands until such times as you shall be, by the said Commissioners, appointed to pay the same unto such treasurer as shall be appointed for the county

Witnesses on the 13th February 1647

Signed George Dodding Thomas Fell

Thomas Rawlinson 1627-89 of Force Forge a Quaker

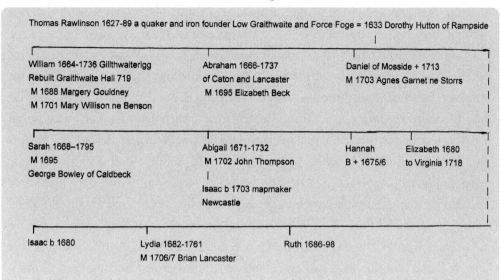

Thomas Rawlinson of Low Graythwaite Hall 1627-1687

Thomas was the eldest son of William Rawlinson the militia captain. Thomas became a Quaker.. Because he had become a quaker he was banned from his father's house for many years, but seems to have been reconciled as he inherited Low Graythwaite. He was certainly paying a substantial assessment in 1685 for the Satterthwaite poor fund. The assessment list usually starts with a Sandys followed by a Rawlinson with nearly the same amount. The succession runs William- Thomas – William from 1652-1707. This place, high in the list, is for Rawlinson of Graythwite. Other Rawlinsons including Grizedale are further down, There is a little bit less for Grizedale and much less for John Rawlinson of the Rolls Office and Abraham of Lancaster. Thomas married at a Quaker ceremony in 1663, Dorothy daughter of Thomas Hutton of Rampside. They had the following children William, Abraham, Daniel, Sarah, Abigail and Lydia. Thomas was for a time a small holder and steward of an estate.

Force Forge was built by 1616. Half of the freehold was bought by William Wright in 1621 In 1658 he sold it to George Fell who also bought the other moiety from Thomas Massarke of Cartlane, Lancs gentleman. George Fell was the only son of Judge Thomas Fell of Swarthmoor Hall. Later that year Judge Fell died. Thomas Rawlinson was working at Force Forge for the Fells from 1658 to 1663 and was soon involved in a dispute with Margaret.Fell who was the judge's widow. George Fell granted Force Forge to his sisters Sarah Fell, Mary Lower nee Fell wife of Thomas Lower, Susan Fell and Rachel Fell in 1666. By 1681 Force Forge had come into the hands of Thomas Lower and Mary who was a sister of Susan, Rachel and George. They sold it to Thomas Rawlinson. This was after a dispute between Rawlinson and the Fell sisters regarding the accounts. In 1680 Thomas had hired John Mattocks a hammer man from Cartmel to work at Force Forge for the rest of his life. In 1684 he promised to pay William Pepper of Preston and John Simpson of Flookburgh gentlemen 20/- before the end of his life. His estate involved :- capital messuage and lands in Graythwaite, messuage and lands in Cunsey alias Cimsacke, messuage and lands in High Wray and Low Wray, iron furnace called Force Forge and land in Ulverston. In 1686 Thomas is selling quarters of iron to Thomas Preston of Holker. After Thomas' death it passed to his son William. Thomas also had an interest in the forge and ironworks at Cunsey which he passed on to his son William in 1688

Thomas was a close friend of George Fox. He with Robert Withers declared against the false worship in the steeple house and was attacked by the common people with loss of blood. In 1656 while traveling in Devonshire on Quaker business Thomas was arrested and sent to prison in Exeter, charged with being a vagabond travelling without a pass. In the same year he was sent to prison for speaking in church and interrupting the priest. In 1659 he was one of 164 Quakers who gathered at Westminster Hall and offered themselves in exchange for the imprisoned London Quakers of which there were 144 in prison; 21 had already died. In 1660 in company with other Quakers he was imprisoned in Lancaster Castle. In 1683 he was fined for attending a Quaker meeting at George Satterthwaites at High Wray. He was buried at Colthouse

Isaac Thompson 1703-1776

The son of Abigail Rawlinson daughter of the preceding by John Thompson of Pool Bar near Crook in Westmorland. He went to work in London but soon moved to Newcastle. With William Cuthbert he founded the "Newcastle Journal" which he edited and printed till his death. He was also a surveyor and produced maps of Newcastle and other North Country areas. He produced two books of poetry one in 1737 to which his cousins Abraham, Isaac and Ebenezer Rawlinson subscribed. He also produced " Natural and experimental philosophy, mechanical, hydrostatic and pneumatic". Obviously a man of many parts. He may have married Rachel Maude, a sister of Warren Maude of Sunderland one of the creditors of Thomas Abraham of Swarthmoor Hall

William Rawlinson of Graythwaite eldest son of Thomas Rawlinson by Dorothy Hutton who died 1736

William obviously inherited Force Forge from his father. In 1710 with John Matchell he had control of Hackett Forge in Little Langdale. In the same year he and John Matchell of Haverthwaite took a years lease on a forge at Coniston with houses, work tools and material from Alice Fleming of Rydal for £41. In 1711 with John Matchell and two others Stephen Crossfield of Plumpton and John Olivant of Penrith who shared a third interest he formed the Backbarrow Co of which Force Forge was one of the assets. William managed the business of the company. In 1716 Crossfield agreed to let Rawlinson buy Olivant's share. In 1717 he was assisted by Gouldney Rawlinson and William Rawlinson Jr, two of his sons. In 1715 Hackett Forge was leased to the Backbarrow and Cunsey Company. In 1717 he was staying in London because his son William wrote to him concerning the Backbarrow Works and letter was addressed care of Michael

William Rawlinson builder Low Graythwaite Hall

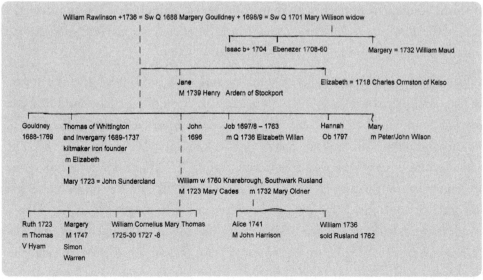

Russell merchant Whitehart Court, Gracious St, London. In 1721 Jo Benson was in London writing to William Rawlinson about Backbarrow works. The Letter is directed via James Garnett, The Royal Oak in Kendal. On the back William has drafted a reply. Partly this concerns his poor son Job who "is honest and no fool but understand indifferently his trade and book-keeping but is too soft and inexperienced to set up for himself." William is also concerned about a lease he and Hales have of iron ore mines in Plain Furness which is due to expire next Candlemass, He is partly concerned because Hales is very friendly with Dumer, the Duke of Montagu's chief steward, and fears they will conspire to keep him out. He wonders if the Duke of Portland can be persuaded to intercede with the Duke of Montagu on his behalf. The Duke of Montagu being Lord of the Manor of Plain Furness. The Backbarrow Company built a second furnace at Leighton Beck near Arnside. The two furnaces were complemented by four forges, Force, Cunsey, Coniston and Backbarrow.

In 1727 they established a furnace at Invergarry in Scotland. The partners were Thomas Rawlinson, William Rawlinson of Graythwaite, William Rawlinson Junior then of Knaresbrough, John Matchell of Haverthwaite, Charles Ormiston of Kelso (married to William's daughter Elizabeth), John Spedding of Whitehaven, Anthony Wilson of High Wray, William Jackson of Yealand and Benjamin Ayrey of Graythwaite. Thomas Rawlinson was the manager. The Rawlinson group also traded in iron products, bacon, cider, cheese and many other items. In 1732 he used his forges at Cunsey, Compston, Hacket, Cartmel and Backbarrow in the wedding settlement of his son William Jr to Mary Oldner. In 1734 he received a letter from R G Sawrey offering to sell him timber for charcoal and suggesting a suitable site for a forge on the River Duddon.

William married twice to Margery Gouldney, and to Mary Willison. By his first wife he had Gouldney, Thomas, William, Job, Hannah, Sarah, Mary, Jane and Elizabeth. By his second wife he had Isaac and Ebenezer. He married Margery daughter of Adam Gouldney clothier and quaker of Chippenham, Wiltshire, in 1688. She had a brother Henry who was of St Clement, East Cheap, London. The marriage settlement has four parties 1/ Thomas Rawlinson and William Rawlinson, his eldest son and heir apparent, 2/ James Hulbert citizen and fishmonger of London, Henry Gouldney merchant of London and Margery Gouldney of Chippenham, spinster. 3/ Roger Sawrey of Broughton Tower and John Rawlinson esquire secretary to the Master of the Rolls 4/ John Whithers citizen and fishmonger of London and

Jeremiah Sawrey of Broughton Tower. Various properties were to be held by the second group till the marriage took place and then to pass to William Rawlinson for life. The properties were Graythwaite Hall, water cornmill and kiln, messuage at Cunsey and Force Forge. Abraham Rawlinson is one of the witnesses. Margery died in 1698/9 and William married Mary who was the widow of Isaac Willison senior of Penrith in 1701 and daughter of Robert Benson, grocer, of Penrith. Her sister Sarah married John Ollivant and her sister Alice George Oldner. . In 1710 William and Mary were involved in a dispute with Mary's son Robert Willison. In 1716 he wrote to his cousin Thomas Richardson a letter about "The grace obtained by Christ for fallen mankind". (Thomas Richardson was presumably the Thomas Richardson of Roanhead who made his will in 1711 and was dead by 1717). regarding a dispute about an estate at Finsthwaite. He arranged with Reginald Gregg to rebuild Graythwaite Hall in 1719. He made a statement of fidelity to the government in 1723 at Hawkshead.

The family also owned Gilthwaitrigge in Skelsiergh. In 1668 William Rawlinson Jnr assigns to his father William Rawlinson of Graythwaite, the militia captain the rents and receipts of the messuage and tenement at Gilthwaitrigge, from whom they descended to William Rawlinson. Who died 1736. In 1712 William Rawlinson of Gilthwaitrigge received from Oliver Martin of the Temple an assurance of his son's title to Graythwaite. In 1712 William Rawlinson wrote from Southwark to Mary Rawlinson of Gilthwaitrigge. In 1717 William Rawlinson of Gilthwaitrigg receives from Robert Wharton a letter about a dispute between Wm and Robert Wharton.

In his will in 1736 he left legacies to his daughters Elizabeth wife of Charles Ormston merchant Kelso and Jane wife of Henry Ardern merchant of Stockport with certain properties listed as a guarantee of payment. The properties were Gillthwaiterigg, Graythwaite, Cunsey fulling mill and land at Force Forge and the George Inn in Penrith. The legacies were paid and the Ormstons and Ardern gave Job Rawlinson a release for the properties .

In 1736 he gave £100 for the school at Colthouse Meeting House.

Connections 1

When William Rawlinson married Margery Gouldney from Chippenham, he married into a nexus of Quaker merchant families. Most previous liaisons had been within 30 miles of Graythwaite. The conversion to Quakerism of Thomas Rawlinson, which his father had thought a disgrace had brought them into a nationwide network. The Quakers were a smallish religious group and were denied entry into many professions and consequently their more energetic and capable members turned to trade and industry. They also kept excellent records.

The Rawlinsons by being included in their in-laws wills and by their younger sons being offered openings, were able to enter into trade business. Margery was the daughter of Adam Gouldney of Chippenham by his wife Jane Hulbert. Margery's brother Henry was a merchant in Cheapside, London and a frequent correspondent of William's. Another brother Adam died in 1698; one sister Mary married Richard Baker, another Quaker merchant often referred to in correspondence, another sister Jane married Michael Russell of Whitehart Court, Gracechurch St. . William Jnr lodged while in London with Henry Gouldny. The Gouldney family of Bristol derived from Chippenham and were much involved in the slave trade. There is no evidence that Margery's immediate family had any involvement with the slave trade or indeed how close they were to the Bristol Gouldneys. Margery's mother Jane was sister of John Hulbert, fishmonger of All Hallows and cousin of James Hulbert, fishmonger of All Hallows who was Master of the Fishmonger's Co and built 20 Almhouses. There is a statue of him near the almshouses. The Hulberts originated in Corsham Wiltshire.

William's sister in law Alice Benson married George Oldner, an upholder in Battersea. in 1696 at Bull & Mouth Quaker Meeting. George's father, George Oldner was a lighterman and his grandfather another George Oldner had invented a device to stop ships foundering and sinking. The lighterman's brother was Sir Richard Oldner a High Sheriff of Surrey. George and Alice had children including Mary who married William Rawlinson Jnr (see below) and George who married Margaret Dickinson who remarried after his death Gabriel Gouldney of the Bristol family. Margaret was the daughter of Caleb Dickinson, by Sarah Vickriss and granddaughter of Francis Dickinson who had served under Cromwell and helped in the capture of Jamaica from the Spaniards was awarded 6000 acres in Jamaica by Charles II. Their estates were Appleton, Barton Island, Pepper,

Watchwell, Delacroix Penn and Cherry Grove. This made them large scale slave owners though most of the family lived in Somerset and used agents to manage the estates. Francis Dickinson had two sons; Jonathan born in Jamaica who moved to Philadelphia and Caleb who bought Monks Combourne in Somerset. Caleb was father of Margaret and her three brothers, Ezekiel of Laycock Hall, Wiltshire, Caleb of Kings Weston, Somerset and Vickriss of Queen Carlton, Somerset. They were all slave owners relying on agents to supervise their estates in Jamaica. Vickriss's will uses the phrase after listing his landed property; he refers to "negroes, horses, beasts and cattle". Clearly these human beings were regarded as so much livestock. Caleb Jnr in his will made sufficient provision to enable Margaret to keep a carriage and live genteely.

The Dickinsons were Quakers, leaving the movement when the Quakers turned against slavery. There is also recorded in Jamaica a Caleb Dickinson, a free gentleman of colour nephew of Robert Hugh Munro also a free gentleman of colour; both were unmarried Munro left a will in 1797 leaving his estate to Dickinson. Dickinson was educated at Catterick, Yorkshire England and was known as Dr Dickinson. He owned Knockpatrick estate and it is claimed he was a grandson of Francis Dickinson which seems unlikely but he may have been a more remote descendant. He also owned Maggotty estate and Grosmont. Caleb Dickinson in his will in 1821 freed his housekeeper Margaret Campbell Dickinson. He also freed five children; Alexander, John, Euan, Henrietta and Elizabeth of James Macpherson by Joan Dickinson. Joan Dickinson was not freed.. He and his uncle between them founded a school for poor children and Munro College

Thomas Rawlinson son of the preceding 1689-1734

Thomas was born in 1689. Thomas is said to have conformed to the Church of England in 1734. This might have entitled him to possession of Whittington Hall under the will of John Rawlinson of Grays Inn his grandfather's brother. He certainly acquired Whittington Hall at some stage. In 1709 he is selling iron to Humphrey Senhouse of Millom. In 1727, on behalf of himself and his partners, Thomas, then living at Whittington Hall, signed a contract with John Macdonell of Invergarry to lease for thirty one years the three merk land of Letterfearn and the five merk land of Invergarry including Invergarry Castle, (up till then Macdonnell's residence, known as "Rock of The Ravens"), with right to use whatever vehicles, to cut whatever timber and to do all things necessary to establish and use an iron works For this he paid £320 down plus 12/- a year for the term of the lease. The attraction of Invergarry was the timber for charcoal. A lot of money was spent improving the infrastructure, such as roadways. He employed a number of locals in the works. He became fond of Highland dress. He wore it in the neatest form. He thought it no great stretch of invention to abridge the dress and make it convenient for his workmen and accordingly directed the use of the lower part plaited or what is called the felie or kilt. The upper part was dispensed with. The result was called the little kilt or felie beg. It was also shorter having been in its previous form ankle length. His workers had from time to time gone up in flames working with furnaces and hot metal.. The shorter kilt was much safer. Its convenience commended it and it was widely adopted. All kilts were banned after the 1745 rebellion but were gradually reintroduced and legalised chiefly in the form of Rawlinson's invention. Despite this there was a fair amount of anti English feeling. One man attempted to murder an English workman but failed as a lowland Scot went to the Englishman's aid and was killed instead. On another occasion Rawlinson was entertaining a number of locals at Rock of The Ravens, a property he had much improved and referred to as his house, to which they took exception and trashed the place. Rawlinson built himself a new house and let Macdonell have the castle back. The enterprise folded after seven years, although the charcoal was cheap all the other costs were great and Rawlinson suffered a lot by constant thefts and other harassments. He died very shortly after his return to England..

In 1734 he is in dispute with his relatives his brothers Job, William, Gouldney and Ebenezer Rawlinson and his sisters Elizabeth Ormston, Jane Harderen, Margery Maud and also with William Williamson, Robert Chambers, John Wilson and a Sawrey. He claimed he had a right to inherit Graythwaite.

He had one daughter Mary born at Whittington in 1721 who married John Sunderland of All Hallows and later of Whittington. John and his brother Thomas of Bigland were involved in various partnerships with the Rawlinsons and others in the iron foundry and furnaces of the area. John and Mary's son Thomas 1744-1809 sold Whittington and bought Littlecroft in Ulverston. Thomas was a leading figure in the promotion of the Ulverston Canal and dug the first sod. He also organized a troupe of volunteers during the Napoleonic wars. Sunderland Terrace in Ulverston is named after him. His son John was vicar of both Ulverston and Pennington and his son George Henry Carlton Sunderland built Swarthdale House now a care home. One of the administrators of Thomas's will was his principal creditor Isaac Rawlinson inn holder of Lancaster. This Isaac Rawlinson had the Sun Inn in Lancaster,frequently used for hearing bankruptcy cases. In 1746 Isaac made a disposition to the government forces identifying one Burton as a Jacobite spy for Bonnie Prince Charlie. His son Isaac Jnr also an innholder, married Margaret Fell of Ulverston at Pennington.

William Rawlinson buried 1760 brother of the proceeding

In 1718 he was at Backbarrow when he sent his father a report on the work at Backbarrow Iron works. He sent the letter care of Michael Russell merchant of Whitehart Court, Gracious St London. Gracious St is close to Fenchurch St where another branch of the Rawlinsons had carried on business as vintners. . In 1723 he married Mary daughter of Cornelius and Ruth Cades of Knaresbrough. In the marriage settlement his father handed over half of his moiety of the ironworks held to be worth £2250, Cornelius offered £1150 three months after the marriage. In the event he only paid £500 before his death.

His widow Ruth took over the running of the family brewery in Knaresbrough and sent another £500. When Mary was expecting her first child, presumably the Ruth who married Thomas Vitriss Hyam at Rookhow Quakers in 1765, her mother Ruth Cades came to Lancashire on a visit complaining about the difficulties of running the brewery and the need for a competent manager. William was persuaded to take the post. It did not work out well.

In 1730 he wrote to the Lord Chancellor complaining about the behavior of his mother in law Ruth Cades. Her brother Boswell Middleton and Boswell Middleton's son Joseph Middleton, which last had married William's sister in law Ruth Cades. In 1733 he sued Joseph and Ruth Middleton.

He was in Knaresbrough at least seven years. He and Mary had three sons William, Cornelius and Thomas and a daughter Mary all born between 1725 and 1730 and all dead by 1731. He found his mother in law and sister in law, Ruth very extravagant and not above removing money from the business. He put his own money in to pay bills and did not receive his due salary. Added to which his mother in law's brother Boswell Middleton was meddling in the business and as a guardian of the younger Ruth, arranged her marriage to his son Joseph. William objected on the grounds of the undesirability of cousin marriage. The promises his mother in law made were not fulfilled, indeed could not be as under the will of Cornelius Cades, his widow only had a life interest and everything went to the younger daughter Ruth, and William's wife Mary was not mentioned at all

He bought Rusland Hall from his Uncle Abraham in 1732/3, who had inherited under his grandfather's will. He married in 1732 Mary Oldner daughter of George Oldner upholder and Quaker of Battersea by his wife Alice. William and Mary had children William 1636 and Alice 1651.

While he was at Rusland he was a partner in the Backbarrow iron foundry with John Matchell of Staveley and James Matchell of Hollow Oak. On 6 5 1735 he and the Matchells came to an agreement with Edward Hall of Cranage in Cheshire gentleman, Warine Falkner esquire of Rugeley Staffs, Thomas Cotton of Eardley Staffs gentleman and Edward Kendall of Stourbridge, Worcestershire concerning iron work owned by the two companies viz:- Cunsey Forge, Curnsey Furnace, Sparkbridge Forge, Leighton Furnace, Backbarrow Furnace and Force Forge all in Lancashire. In 1735 there is a lease from Sir William Fleming of Rydal of Coniston Forge to William Rawlinson of Rusland Hall, John Matchell of Bigland Hall, Edward Hall of Cranage and James Matchell of Haverthwaite. On 10/5/1745 they joined with Edward Kendall, Edward Hall and Thomas Colton partners in Cunsey iron foundry to appoint as trustees for Nibthwaite iron foundry Benjamin Ayrey, Edward Kendall and William Lathom. Later (before 1750) William Rawlinson withdrew conveying his interest to John Matchell, and James Matchell, James Matchell and Thomas Matchell as executor for John Matchell deceased.

William moved about a bit in the course of his life. In 1713 he was of Southwark when he wrote to Mary Rawlinson at Gilthwaite Rigg. He was apprenticed in 1714 to John Chaytor of Dublin. And he was in London in 1723. He was of Bigland in 1724 but in 1725 he had moved to Knaresbrough. In 1726 he received two letters one from Benjamin Ayres about the Backbarrow Works while staying with Widow Gouldney in Clemens Lane and the other while staying at John Bell's in Clemens Lane, London. He was back in Knaresbrough in 1733 when he brought a suit against Joseph Middleton and his wife Ruth. He was called Jr at the time. He bought Rusland Hall in 1732/3 and was of that place in his will proved 1760. He was of Rusland in 1749 when his brother Job sold him his shares in Backbarrow Iron Works. He was there in 1752 when he had a suit with John Walker. On the other hand he was described as of Bank Side, St Saviour Southwark in his brother in law, George Oldner of Stockwell's will of 1735. In 1757 he renounces claim to house in Golders Green, Temple Fortune.

By his wife Mary Cades he had several children in Knaresbrough, Mary, William, Cornelius and Thomas who all died young and Ruth who was born in Hawkshead parish and married Thomas Vickris Hyam a merchant of London. By his wife Mary Oldner he had children William and Alice. Alice married John Harris a London merchant.

Rusland Hall

Connections 2

Thomas Vickris Hyam was the son of Thomas Hyam by Ann Vickriss.

Thomas Hyam was a prominent Quaker merchant and a friend of the Penn family owning land in Philadelphia. He was approached by Benjamin Franklin among others, along with Sylvanus Bevan, apothecary of Hackney to help find land for a hospital in Pennsylvania. They did make an offer which wasn't taken up. He was banker for the Bristol merchant Graffin Pankard who was father in law of the younger Caleb Dickinson. Thomas and Ruth had nine children including Thomas Rawlinson Hyam.

Ann Vickris was daughter of Richard Vickris a quaker writer son of Robert Vickris MP. Her sister Sarah married Caleb Dickenson the elder (see above Connections 1).

Sylvanus Bevan was an apothecary. An executor of his will in 1765 was Christopher Rawlinson of Hackney and Coombe in Hampshire, who was no connection of the Rawlinsons of Graythwaite but an ancestor of Lord Rawlinson of Ewall. The apothecary business was continued by Sylvanus's brother, Timothy, and descendants, a former apprentice of theirs a Mr Allen founded the company now known as Glaxo Smith Klein

Job Rawlinson brother of the preceding 1697/8-1763

Job married Elizabeth Willan who died in 1768. He was a Quaker. He had two sons William and Robert. William 1740 -1808 married Catherine Waldie by whom he had John Job, Robert and William. In 1746 with William Crossfield, Isaac Wilkinson and George Drinkall Job created the Lowood Company with furnace and forge. Two years later Wilkinson and Drinkall left and were replaced by Thomas Sunderland. The company was taken into the Backbarrow group in 1784. He was involved in setting up a company a forge and ironworks at Cunsey in 1747 . On 16th October 1747, he, with William Crossfield of Cartmel, George Drinkall of Rusland and John Coulson of Rusland joined George Braithwaite and Richard Taylor yeomen of Finsthwaite, John Lindow of Cartmell Fell yeoman and John Wilson yeoman of Hawkshead in setting up a company at the works at Low Wood. At the same time he with William Crossfield, George Drinkall and Isaac Wilkinson leased Low Wood estate forge and furnace from George Bigland

Job Rawlinson of Lowood Forge and Furnace

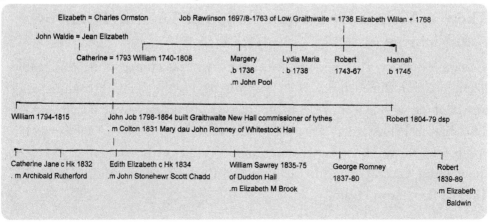

for 51 years. In 1748 he handed his interest in Force Forge to William Crossfield of Seatle Cartmell and George Drinkall of Rusland . In 1749 he sells land and property in Ulverston and Hawkshead to William Crossfield, George Drinkall, John Dodgson and Simon Wilkinson and was joined in the sale by Peter Wilson and his wife Mary and Thomas Richardson and his wife Margaret Rawlinson. He was a freeman of the City of Lancaster as was his son William. In 1758 he borrowed £200 from the Colthouse Meeting. In 1694 his father had left £100 to Hawkshead school in two tranches. This money was lent to Job who paid £2 to the school and £2 to the schoolmaster per year as interest on the loan.

John Job Rawlinson of Graythwaite New Hall 1798 - 1864

John Job Rawlinson was son of William Rawlinson died in 1808 and grandson of Job Rawlinson. He built Graythwaite New Hall in 1820. I rather think this is the building now known as Silverholme. In fact in Silverholme there is a staircase window dedicated to the Rawlinson family. Graythwaite Low Hall is a separate building built by William Rawlinson 1719. The whole Rawlinson estate was taken over by the Sandys family, long time neighbours who still own it. Silverholme and Graythwaite Low Hall are both let out for holidays and Silverholme is a wedding venue (see Graythwaite Estate web site for pictures) John Job also owned Duddon Hall. He married Mary daughter of John Romney and they had the following children;- Catherine Jane, Edith Elizabeth, William Sawrey, George Romney and Robert. He was a freeman of the City of Lancaster. He was a barrister and in 1861 an assistant tythe and enclosure commissioner. As far as I can see he has no surviving male line descendants.

Low Graythwaite Hall   **Silverholme**

William Sawrey Rawlinson of Duddon Hall

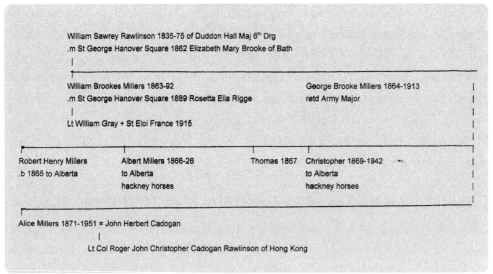

William Sawrey Rawlinson 1835-75 of Duddon Hall Maj 6ᵗʰ Drg
.m St George Hanover Square 1862 Elizabeth Mary Brooke of Bath

William Brookes Millers 1863-92	George Brooke Millers 1864-1913
.m St George Hanover Square 1889 Rosetta Ella Rigge	retd Army Major
Lt William Gray + St Eloi France 1915	

Robert Henry Millers	Albert Millers 1866-26	Thomas 1867	Christopher 1869-1942
.b 1865 to Alberta	to Alberta		to Alberta
	hackney horses		hackney horses

Alice Millers 1871-1951 = John Herbert Cadogan

Lt Col Roger John Christopher Cadogan Rawlinson of Hong Kong

William Sawrey Rawlinson 1837-96

Eldest son of John Job Rawlinson resided at Duddon Hall married Edith Brooks and had five sons and a daughter;- William Brooks Millers 1863-92, George Brooks Millers 1864-1913, Robert Henry Millers 1865, Arthur Millers 1866, Christopher Millers 1869 and Alice Millers 1873,

Revd George Millers had inherited Duddon Hall and left it to any of the Rawlinsons who adopted the name Millers in addition to their own.

In 1882 Arthur and Christopher emigrated to Alberta in Canada taking a ranch on the Bow Rivers, 11 miles north of Calgary. They took four hackney horses with them and imported others. They were quite successful, giving up the ranch in 1907 when they returned to England. They later emigrated to Barbados and bought a rum factory. This they gave up in 1909 spending the summers in Alberta and the winters in Barbados. Arthur died in 1926, Christopher in 1942, Neither of these two were married. Robert also had a ranch in Alberta. He did marry and had a son William Henry who in turn had a son Kenneth Henry who died at 16 in 1936 and was the last male in the line.

Duddon Hall formerly Duddon Grove had been built by Richard Towers, son of Thomas Towers of Bouth by his wife Frances Robinson. He inherited the estate on which it was built from his uncle John Robinson attorney of Ulverston who died in 1803. He built soon after inheriting. He died in 1831. He left it to his niece Frances Esther Millers daughter of Revd William Millers, fellow St John's College Cambridge. She left it to her father who in turn left it to his brother Revd George Millers, a minor canon of Ely Cathedral. William and George were the sons of Thomas Millers, hatter of Kendal by his wife Esther Abbott a sister of Mary Abbott, wife of the artist George Romney. John Job Rawlinson married a granddaughter of the Romneys which was presumably why one of his family inherited Duddon Hall. William Brooks Millers Rawlinson was of Duddon Hall most of his life. He married Rosetta Rigges in St George's, Hanover Square in London. She was a descendant of the Cark line. Their son William Gray was at Duddon Hall in 1891 while his parents were visiting John Rawlinson Ford at Yealand. William Gray Rawlinson was killed at St Eloi in World War I, he was a lieutenant in the Duke of Cornwall's regiment.

Robert Rawlinson of Graythwaite died Cheltenham 1838-1889

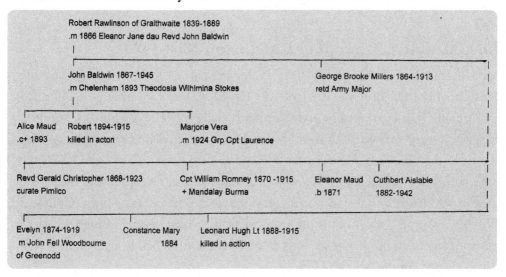

John Baldwin Rawlinson of Graythwaite Hall 1867-1945

He was the son of Robert Rawlinson (third son of John Job) by Eleanor Jane Baldwin daughter of Revd John Baldwin. She was a cousin being descended from the Romneys. John Baldwin Rawlinson married at Cheltenham in 1893 Theodosia Wilhelmina Stokes. John Rawlinson was a cricketer, but not a very good one, playing once in first class cricket for Oxford University and not doing very well then.. He got into financial difficulties and was unable to pay his debts. In 1905 he sold the Graythwaite Estate to Colonel T M Sandys. Relations with his wife deteriorated and they lived apart. There is a letter from his mother in law asking for access to her grandchildren. In 1906 he hired Charles Richard a detective to gather evidence of his wife's affair with John George Mclean one of the mortgagees of Graythwaite estate. His wife found out, no divorce ensued and neither party was able to remarry. In 1939 there is a letter from M Stokes saying that there is some property at Graythwaite belonging to Mrs Rawlinson and hoping it has been protected from seizure. He states "Mr Rawlinson is behaving in a most shameful manner" Rawlinson made his will at the United Universities Club Pall Mall London in 1937. It was proved in 1945. There were three children of the marriage Alice Maud born and died 1893 Robert 1894-1915, was a lieutenant in the 2 nd Border Regiment. He was klled in WWI 10th May 1915, his body was never found and his name is on the Loos Memorial at Dud Corner Cemetary, as well as on a plaque in Finsthwaite Church, and Marjory Vera Rawlinson who married Frederick Laurence 1947 in Bombay

Revd Gerald Christopher Rawlinson 1868-1923

A brother of John Baldwin Rawlinson. He was part of the Affirming Catlholic Movement in the Church of England. He served as curate at St Barnabas, Pimlico a church built to express in its architecture the beliefs of the Affirming Catholics, He gave lectures on Meditation and Mysticism. A large monument depicting him stands in the church in his memory. He and John Baldwin Rawlinson had three other brothers. Wilfred Romney was a captain in the Liverpool Regiment, he died in 1915 at Mandalay in Burma presumably not by enemy action. Cuthbert Aislabie who spent most of his life in an institution and Leonard Hugh who was a lieutenant in the 2nd Border Regiment was killed 10th May 1915 near Ypres and is named on the Menim Gate

RAWLINSON OF LANCASTER AND CHADLINGTON

Abraham Rawlinson of Caton, Lancaster and Melling merchant and iron founder

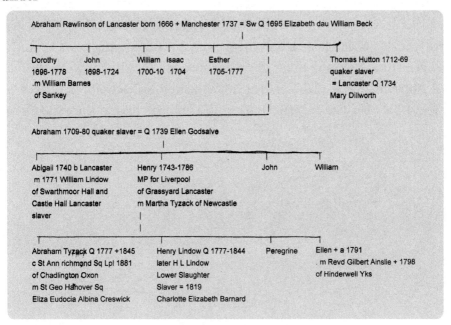

Abraham Rawlinson of Lancaster born 1666 + Manchester 1737 = Sw Q 1695 Elizabeth dau William Beck

Dorothy	John	William	Isaac	Esther		Thomas Hutton 1712-69
1696-1778	1698-1724	1700-10	1704	1705-1777		quaker slaver
.m William Barnes						= Lancaster Q 1734
of Sankey						Mary Dilworth

Abraham 1709-80 quaker slaver = Q 1739 Ellen Godsalve

Abigail 1740 b Lancaster	Henry 1743-1786	John	William
m 1771 William Lindow	MP for Liverpool		
of Swarthmoor Hall and	of Grassyard Lancaster		
Castle Hall Lancaster	m Martha Tyzack of Newcastle		
slaver			

Abraham Tyzack Q 1777 +1845	Henry Lindow Q 1777-1844	Peregrine	Ellen + a 1791
c St Ann richmond Sq Lpl 1881	later H L Lindow		. m Revd Gilbert Ainslie + 1798
of Chadlington Oxon	Lower Slaughter		of Hinderwell Yks
m St Geo Hanover Sq	Slaver = 1819		
Eliza Eudocia Albina Creswick	Charlotte Elizabeth Barnard		

Abraham Rawlinson of Lancaster 1666-1737

Abraham was the second son of Thomas Rawlinson the Quaker of Force Forge.

He was born in 1666 and married Elizabeth daughter of William Beck of Low Wray in 1695. Their children were Dorothy 1696 who married William Barnes, John 1698, William 1700, Isaac 1701, Esther 1705, Abraham 1709 and Thomas Hutton 1712. His wife's sister Hester died on what was to be her wedding day in 1687.She was going to marry William Grave of Broadgate in Westmorland. As he was thought to have been a scoundrel the opinion at the time was that Hester was well out of it. Abraham was assessed for the Satterthwaite poor rate for a mill in their area in 1701. In 1702 he was the first named of a committee of nine empowered by Colthouse Meeting to enlarge the graveyard and to provide a place of ease at the back end of the Meeting House. All Abraham's children were born in Furness after which he moved to Lancaster and became a merchant. He established an iron forge at Caton near Lancaster in 1727. His two youngest sons were very much involved in the West India Trade, though there is no actual evidence that he was as well. He was in the iron foundry trade and acquired mining rights at Lindal and Dalton in Furness in 1745. He acquired Rusland Hall after the death of his Uncle John Rawlinson under the will of his grandfather William Rawlinson and buying out John's widow Mrs Mary Rawlinson of St Martin in the Fields. . He sold 12 acres of peat moss in Rusland Heights to Clement Taylor and Myles Harrison in 1726. He kept a bull for servicing neighbouring cows at Rusland Hall. Clement Taylor took a cow there six times in 1731. In 1733/4 by lease and release Abraham sold Rusland Hall etc to William Rawlinson Jnr of Graythwaite Hall for £1800 . He died at Manchester in 1737 though his residence was Hornby.

Excursus 6
Slavery

Slavery was until fairly recent times an almost universal vice. Certainly West Africa the source of most of the slaves transported to the Americas, had institutionalized slavery many centuries before any European set foot in the area. The three empires of Ghana, Mali and Sonjhay all practiced slavery. In the late 17th and 18th centuries the Europeans bought the slaves from the Africans. The slaves were prisoners of war from inter tribal warfare. It is of course possible that the willingness of Europeans to buy the slaves encouraged some Africans to kidnap members of other tribes for this specific purpose. The conditions on board the slave ships while the prisoners were being transported to the Americas was appalling and disease was rife. Many of the prisoners died and a fair number of the crew. Ordinary sailors much preferred to go whaling. There was a much better chance of coming back alive. The only Rawlinson, so far that I know was involved in buying slaves in Africa and transporting them across the Atlantic was Richard Rawlinson's unsatisfactory nephew, Thomas (see above). Two of Abraham of Caton and Hornby's sons Abraham and Thomas Hutton were involved in trading from England to the Carribean and by the end of their lives owned estates in the islands and the slaves who worked on them. They both mentioned negroes in their wills. Thomas Hutton's son Abraham Rawlinson MP was a vigorous defender of slavery but doesn't actually mention them in his will. However his nephew Abraham Rawlinson, banker of Fakenham, was a beneficiary when slave owners were compensated in 1833. Abraham MP had a cousin Henry son of his uncle Abraham who was also a MP but died young. His son Abraham Tysack Rawlinson set himself up as a landed gentleman in Oxford-shire partly helped by revenues from slave estates. Established merchants such as the Rawlinsons were likely to concentrate on trading with the West Indies buying cotton, coffee and sugar as well as shipping their own produce to England and selling to the West Indies a lot of manufactured goods. The business of sailing to Africa and buying slaves and transporting them to the Americas was a lot riskier both financially and in terms of personal health and was left to smaller merchants trying to get themselves established.

The various stages of slavery:

    1/ The capture and enslavement of individuals and groups

    2/ The sale of these captives to traders or would be slave owners

    3/ The transportation of slaves across the Atlantic

    4/ The sale of these slaves to owners of plantations, etc

    5/ The employment of slaves on the plantations

    6/ Alternatively new slaves could be sold on to other islands or to America.

After this the slaves either died due to hard work and poor conditions or survived and entered into relationships with other slaves and produced children who were born into slavery. Meanwhile the produce of the plantations was sold for consumption in Europe. Some Lancaster traders were engaged in the slave trade, that is, they sent or took ships out to West Africa, were the purchasers in item 2/ the agents in 3/ and the vendors in 4/. Those merchants in the West India Trade bought the produce of the plantations to sell in Europe and took European products to Africa to sell there. They might buy plantations in which case they became owners of the slaves on the plantations. They sent out agents to help sell the cargoes they sent out and buy in the cotton, coffee or sugar for the return trip or manage the estates they had bought. This is what the Rawlinsons of Lancaster did. I suspect the money from the family iron forging business helped get them established in the West India trade but cannot prove it. The only Rawlinson know to be involved in the slave trade as such that is 2/ to 4/ above was from a different branch of the family and was the Thomas Rawlinson mentioned above. However the Rawlinsons and possibly other West India Merchants did engage in 6/ In 1752 the "Providence" took 20 slaves to Carolina from Barbados. She was owned by the brothers Abraham and Thomas Hutton Rawlinson, two Dilworths and two others. In 1786 Thomas Rawlinson's ship "Abbey" transported 180 slaves from St Vincent to Tobago.

Chronology

22 June 1772 Mansfield Judgment which asserted slavery was impossible in Britain without primary legislation, of which there was none, thus making all slaves in Britain free.

1808 Slave trading illegal in United Kingdom after which the British Navy took action to suppress slave trading world wide.

1833 Slave owning illegal throughout British Empire

Quaker opinions with regard to the morality of slavery

It is often said that the Quakers were opposed to slavery. Yet they seemed able to cope with it among their members in the early to middle eighteenth century. They were much keener on pacifism and decent behavior. Persistent failure to attend meeting was ground for expulsion as was a disorderly life style, marrying a non Quaker and any involvement with fighting. It wasn't until 1792 that they took issue with Thomas Rawlinson about his involvement with slavery

Rawlinson estates

Thomas Hutton Rawlinson's son Thomas had estates in St Vincent, Grenada, Broom Hall, Berbice and Demerara. The last two are what is now Guyana, formerly British Guiana but before that Berbice and Demerara were in the Dutch West Indies. There was a slave revolt in Berbice in 1763 which lasted a good twelve months before it was suppressed. Most of the plantations involved were on the banks of the River Berbice not on the coast. The plantations in which Thomas Rawlinson had a minority share were on the coast and the chief owner was Thomas Bond followed by his nephew John Bond. One plantation was called Lancaster. As the British took this area at the end of the 18th century .and they were the ones who developed the coastal areas Lancaster might not have existed many years before 1800.

Lydia Rawlinson Lancaster 1683-1761

The youngest daughter of Thomas Rawlinson the Quaker. She was brought up in the Society of Friends.. She was called to ministry at the age of fourteen but resisted till she was twenty four. She married Brian Lancaster in 1707 and began her ministry in 1708 . She travelled locally and to London, Ireland and Scotland

and in 1718-19 went with a party, including her sister in law, Elizabeth Beck Rawlinson to America. For a while she lived at Colthouse near Hawkshead with her widowed mother but eventually moved to Lancaster where she died. In 1840 Lydia Ann Barclay a descendent of Thomas Hutton Rawlinson (great nephew to Lydia) published some of Lydia writings including an account of her call to ministry and a selection of letters.

Abraham Rawlinson 1709-80

Abraham was the fourth son of the previous Abraham. He was a West India Merchant with his brother Thomas Hatton Rawlinson. .In 1736 he was sent out to the West Indies to look after the family's interests. In 1739 with Benjamin Satterthwaite as his asssistant, he was the firm's agent in Barbados. The firm in question was probably the one lead by Miles Townson and in which Abraham and his brother Thomas Hutton were partners. On 28th September 1740 Satterthwaite writes "Abraham Rawlinson wrote to a man on this island that he intends to be here by the latter end of September which will prove true. He has given me a strange sort of character here as well as at home, but I believe that he got no good will from the people here with it. I desire that you would not mention this ever again. I desire I may have no more concerns with him than to liver up my work here. If I should be obliged to stay four or more weeks after his arrival. Mrs Duke has offered me a room to myself where I may put my desk while I collect the remainder of my debts which is the needful" What the problem was is likely to remain a mystery. Benjamin seems to have got on better with Thomas Hutton Rawlinson. In 1740 Abraham Rawlinson with Myles Birkett and James Stockdale of Cartmel obtained mining rights in Lindal and Dalton, indicating that he had not abandoned the family iron foundry business. Between 1752 and 1762 they had more ships registered at Liverpool than any other Lancaster traders. In the 1760s they acquired the Goyave Plantation in Grenada. There is a portrait by Romney in Lancaster Museum commissioned by his son in law William Lindow. He married in a Quaker ceremony in 1739 Ellen Godsalve. They had the following children :- Abigail 1740, Henry1743, John 1744 of Newcastle, William of Manchester, Thomas 1752 of Yealand and Abraham 1757. From 1750-55 and again 1758-61 and again from 1770 Abraham was a member of the Port Commission of Lancaster and was much involved with the building of a quay. He and Miles Birkett arranged for the necessary act of parliament. The Port Commision appointed William

Thornton to be Pier Master and Collector of taxes and dues. He was presumably a relation of the William Thornton mentioned below. .

Abraham and his brother Hutton arranged for John Lettsome to lodge with their sister Dorothy wife of William Barnes of Great Sankey while he was trained in Penketh. Lettsome was born on Tortola to a Quaker family and was escorted to England by William Lindow (agent, future son in law of Abraham). Lettsome went on to become a famous doctor. This makes me wonder about William Thornton, whose father was a plantation owner on Tortola and who was sent to relatives in Lancaster who placed him as an apprentice with Dr John Fell, the Quaker doctor in Ulverston. Thornton went on to design the Capitol Building in Washington while working as a doctor. Thornton and Lettsome were friends. The relatives of Thornton who were Quakers were Margaret Birket Thornton of Caton his grandmother and his uncle James Birkett.. William Barnes was born in 1690 in Great Sankey son of William Barnes and his wife nee Elizabeth Cobham. Williams grandfather another William 1620-1679 had the largest house in Great Sankey with nine hearths at the Hearth Tax in 1666. Previously in 1646 he had been one of two lay elders of the newly built Presbyterian Chapel in Great Sankey. He was visited by George Fox,(who seems to have targeted non conformist gentry) and became a Quaker. His house was used for meetings of the Quakers up to 1681when a meeting house was built. William married Dorothy Rawlinson in 1727. A list of poor law officials for the time lists William Barnes many times as constable, overseer of the poor and supervisor of the highways. It is possible we are dealing with three separate William Barnes as they are described as of Sefton House, of Cow Lane House and as of his own house. However Dorothy Barnes was constable in 1762 when of Cow Lane House.

John Lettsome freed all his slaves when he attained his majority at 21. William Thornton admired him for this and thought of freeing his own slaves but never got round to it. Most if not all of his slaves belonged to his wife, which may be an explanation.

Abraham was a freeman of the City of Lancaster as were his sons John, William, Thomas and Samuel

Abraham Rawlinson

Abraham and his brother Thomas Hutton were regular worshipers at the Society of Friends. Whatever the Quakers thought of Slavery these two and others managed a devotion to Quakerism and a wholehearted and wide ranging involvement in the slave trade.

He specifically refers to negroes as among his possessions in his will in 1779 there is a note in the minutes of the local Quakers in 1779 referring to the dismemberment of this Abraham and his son Thomas. However judging from Abraham's indignant reply to the meeting this was an accusation that his ships carried letters of marque which was the way the government sanctioned piracy against foreign ships. Abraham denies the charge. The Quakers in Lancaster were not objecting to his ownership of slaves.

In 1745 he received a letter from Joseph Fisher asking for two tierces (sic)of Sugar and including the following note:- "At a place called Clifton two miles from Penrith a Friend lived there whose name was Thomas Savage. His house lay by the road south and his curtain was filled with the rebel crew in a shallow manner with a design to intercept the small parties of the Duke's army and destroy them. Thomas being in his chamber looks out and Happily spied the army with the Duke in front not far from the house, upon which he let own a boy at the back of the house sending him with the strictest charge to the Duke to acquaint him with the situation of the rebels, whereon the Duke drew up in a proper manner dispersed many and took several prisoners. The Duke tarryed all night with Thomas Savage and will no doubt remember him for being instrumental in such a providential deliverance." Joseph Fisher's English is not exactly modern. The rebels are presumably supporters of Bonnie Prince Charley. The Duke is presumably a member of the governments forces. The story illustrates the hazards of the day.

Abigal Rawlinson Lindow

Abigail was the eldest child of the preceding Abraham Rawlinson. She married William Lindow, a slave trader. There is portrait of them by Romney in Lancaster Museum. They had no children. William Lindow represented the Rawlinsons on St Kitts by the late 1750s moving to Grenada by 1763. William Lindow was on the Governor's Council in Grenada. He captained several vessels used in the West India trade but not in the African slave trade including one called the "Rawlinson". However he did send 77 slaves to Dominica from Grenada in 1766 on the "Hobbey Horse". He ended up owning a considerable estate in Low Furness including Swarthmoor Hall. He also owned plantations on four West Indian Islands. When he returned to England and married Abigail they lived in Lancaster. They are buried in the parish church graveyard

Henry Rawlinson MP for Liverpool 1743-86

Henry was the eldest son of Abraham Rawlinson 1709-80. He was born 1743

He was MP for Liverpool 1780 -84. In 1781 he opposed the presentation of a petition advocating economic reform. He supported Lord North's administration but in 1782 voted with the opposition to censure Lord Sandwich's conduct of naval affairs. Also in 1782 he defended Cavendish's conduct of matters in the West Indies in a censure debate. In 1783 he voted for Shelborne's peace preliminaries but subsequently went with the coalition. He did not stand in 1784. He married at North Shields Quaker Meeting House 1765 Martha daughter of Peregrine Tysack of Newcastle upon Tyne a glass manufacturer. He owned Grasyard Hall near Lancaster. Their children were Abraham Tysack, Henry Lindow and Peregrine., Marion, Ellen, Elizabeth and Martha. After Henry's death his widow and children continued to live at Grassyard. In March 1791 Ellen Rawlinson (wife of Revd Gilbert Ainslie) one of the daughter's died and a dispute arose between Mrs Rawlinson and Dr Ainslie who was Revd Gilbert Ainslie of Hinderwell who had married the daughter Ellen in November 1790 Evidently while her daughter was dying Mrs Rawlinson had tried to persuade her to leave her (Mrs Rawlinson) some furniture. The dispute also concerned the management of the late daughter's effects. The couple had only been married for four months.. He died in 1792. Gilbert Ainslie's nephew Montague Ainslie built Ford House in Ulverston Another of the Rawlinson daughters Maria married Robert Hesketh and one of their sons was Sir Peter Fleetwood Hesketh MP

Abraham Tysack Rawlinson 1777-1848

Abraham was the eldest son of Henry Rawlinson MP and his wife Martha. He had a twin brother Henry Lindow Rawlinson. His father died when he was 9. He and his brother Henry were sent to Rugby School and then in 1795 to Christ Church Oxford. Although they got degrees their main interests were in sport and social life. He was brought up at Grassyard Lancaster by his mother but while at Oxford developed a dislike of the North Country which led him to sell Grassyard when he came in to the property at 21. For four years from 1800 he lived at Lower Slaughter then for a year at Rangers Lodge Wychwood Forest Oxfordshire. In 1806 he bought Chadlington Oxfordshire an estate of 700 acres with a certain amount of game on it . There he became very much the country squire supervising his own farming, hunting and serving as a guardian of the poor, a justice of the peace and deputy Lieutenant for Oxfordshire which post he held 1805-45 . A Thomas Rollinson was living at Chadlington House while he was High Sherriff of Oxfordshire in 1766 and a William Rollinson was there in the 17th century. Despite the fact that Rollinson and Rawlinson are basically the same name and some families swop from one to the other, in this case there is no connection. There is a deed held by Shakespeare's Birthplace Trust in which Mary Rollinson a coheiress of the Rollinson family sells Chadlington to Abraham Tysack Rawlinson. Abraham Tysack Rawlinson sent his eldest son to Rugby School. Abraham married Eliza Eudocia Albina Creswick daughter of Martin Creswick and they had eleven children altogether including :- Abraham Lindow 1805, Henry Creswick

Abraham Tyzack Rawlinson of Chadlington Oxfordshire

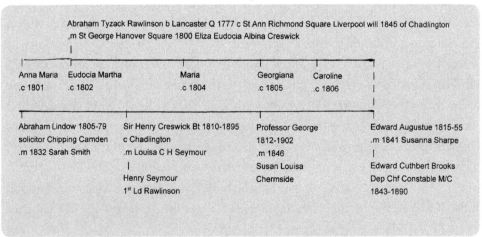

1810, George, Edward Augustus, Maria who married Brooke Smith of Bristol and Georgina. Eliza's sister Anna Eugenia had married Richard Smith a surgeon in Bristol. Because Martin Creswick's only son died young Eliza and Anna inherited £20,000 each. Abraham made about £1200 to £1500 a year out of his farming. He also had land in the West Indies and elsewhere which brought his income up to £2000 a year. Abraham also reared and bred racehorses producing a Derby winner "Coronation" in 1841. The agricultural depression which followed a war in America left him somewhat worse off. He had sent his eldest son to Rugby but could not do the same for his other children,

Sir Henry Creswick Rawlinson Bt 1810-95

Henry was the second son and seventh child of Abraham Tysack Rawlinson. He had five older sisters He was born at Chadlington in Oxfordshire. His elder brother had gone to Rugby school but agricultural depression had reduced family income by Henry's turn. Until he was eleven he was taught by his mother English, Arithmetic and some Latin.

He suffered an ophthalmic attack and according spent some time in Bristol where his mother's brother in law Richard Smith was a surgeon. In the event whether by treatment or happenstance the attack was aborted and his right eye was sound while there remained some sight in his left eye. He attended Dr Pocock's School in Bristol and was introduced to his Aunt's Circle which included Hannah More the writer and a Mrs Schimmelpeninck who taught him a smattering of Hebrew He went to Wrington 1821-1823 and then Ealing.

At 17 he was sent, as a cadet in the army of the East India Company to Bombay, The journey to Bombay by ship took sometime and during the voyage he became acquainted with Sir John Malcolm the Governor General of Bombay a soldier, diplomat and scholar of the orient including the Persian language to which he introduced Rawlinson. While in Bombay he learnt Hindustani and Maharatta. He was a good horseman and a good shot. He was appointed to a regiment then transferred twice finishing with the 1st Bombay Grenadiers. With them he went to Poonah in Guzerat staying there from 1830-1833 where he much enjoyed the life of an aristocratic army officer without losing his interest in the various languages and ancient remains of the area.

In 1833 The East India Company was invited to train the Shah of Persia's army. In fact the aim was to bring them back to the standard of organisation and discipline they had had when they had British officers. Rawlinson was one of those sent to take part in the work.

He was appointed by Lord Clare, Sir John Malcolm's successor as Governor General partly because of his knowledge of Persian, but also because of his friendship with Lord Clare's son Lt Upton. He attended the coronation of Shah Mohammed Mirza. His knowledge of Persian made him much in demand as an interpreter and his honesty in this role meant that he gained the Shah's trust.

In February 1835 The Shah asked him to go to Kirmanshah in Kurdistan a province governed by his brother Bahram Mirza. On the way he passed the ruins of Ecbatana and was attracted by the inscriptions particularly those on Mount Elvand. He transcribed some of these not knowing others had done so before him. While he was in Kirmanshah he raised three regiments of local men as soldiers. He was first drawn to the sculptures at Taicht -I-Bostam but late took an interest in the inscriptions on the rock at Behuistan about 12 miles from Kirmanshah. He set out to transcribe these particularly the Old Persian. The Rock at Behuistan is steep, precipitous in places, yet Rawlinson climbed up it three or four times a day without rope or ladders in order to copy the inscriptions. These are in three languages (Persian, Mede & Elamite) inscription which Darius Hystaspes the Great had inscribed there. During his stay he joined the Royal Asiatic Society. He was based at Kirmanshah.

On one occasion he was sent to the headwaters of the River Kerkhaw to recruit some of the Gurum Kirds to the Shah's military service and assist the Governor of Zohab one Suleiman Khan. He did this but was shortly summoned back to Kirmanshah to await a message from the Shah, while in Kirmanshah the new troops rebelled, killed Suleiman Shah and were heading to the Turkish Border seeking sanctuary.. Barham Mirza decided the only person, capable of resolving the situation was Lt Rawlinson who did in fact return to Zohab managed to secure the person of Mohammed Wali Khan, Suleiman Khan's son and pursued the rebels. He caught them before the border and got them to renew their vows of loyalty to the Shah. He appointed Mohammed Wali Khan in his father's place. This action was endorsed by Bahram Mirza. Rawlinson had been extremely energetic and collapsed with over work.

He returned to Baghdad to a European house and the care of a Dr Ross who not only aided his recovery but began to teach him Arabic, assisted in this by a Captain Taylor. On returning to Zohab he was involved with an expedition with Bahram Mirza to put down a rebel in the Bakhtiari Mountains. However, the rebel hearing of their approach abandoned his rebellion. On the way back Rawlinson chose to return through the mountains of Luristan being the first European to do so.

In the winter of 1836-37 Rawlinson set about copying such portions of the great inscription, at Behuistan, as were accessible to him. He managed to transcribe all the first column, the first paragraph of the second column, 10 paragraphs of the third column and four paragraph of the detached inscriptions. Bahram Mirza fell out of favour with the Shah and was replaced. He and Rawlinson did not get on very well. In due course Rawlinson was recalled to Tehran to give an account of himself to the Shah. On arrival in Tehran he discovered the Shah had set off for Herat, with an army with the intention of invading Herat and if possible capturing it. The British envoy Sir John McNeill, instructed him to follow. He accomplished the ride of 800 miles in a week.

His party was pretty well knocked up and while riding during the last night lost the road and found themselves off the road on the broken plain which stretches up to the hills containing the turquoise mines. They noticed another group of horsemen also apparently trying to recover the high road. They avoided them for safety reasons but noticed some were in Cossack dress and one of Rawlinson's party identified one as a servant at the Russian Mission. Russians had not been seen so far south in Persia before. They arrived at the Khan staging post and went in, the other party hearing that he was a British officer did not enter the Khan. Rawlinson was curious about this and thought he ought to find out more, so he followed them. After a bit they turned off the high road and entered a gorge in the mountains. He followed them and found them settled near a clear mountain stream. A fair haired man was obviously an officer. Rawlinson spoke in French, the officer shook his head. Rawlinson tried English the officer replied in Russian. He then tried Persian the officer replied in Turcoman or Usbeg Turkish of which Rawlinson had enough for a simple conversation but not enough to be inquisitive. This evidently suited the officer. He admitted he was a Russian officer with presents for the Shah.

Rawlinson reached the Shah's camp before dark and after explaining his conduct in Tehran to the satisfaction of the Shah he mentioned his morning encounter. The Shah replied he knew nothing of him but had been asked to help him on his way to Dost Mohammed ruler of Afghanistan at Kabul. The Russians arrived two days later and Rawlinson was introduced to the Russian officer; Captain Vitkievitch who replied in excellent French that it was well to be careful with strangers one met in the desert. Vitkievitch went on to Kabul where he was well received by the Afghan authorities but failed to achieve all he set out to do so that when he returned to St Petersburg he was out of favour and blew his brains out, however his presence in Kabul was one of the things that lead to the outbreak of the Afghan War of 1839-42. It alerted Rawlinson to the long term policy objectives of the Russian Czar and the danger to British interests in India.

In the meantime he was appointed officer in charge of the Shah's arsenal in Tehran. The expedition to Herat was part of the Shah's aggressive policy towards Herat and Afghanistan. The British helped the Afghans fight him off which lead to the departure of the East India Company Army from Persia. The Shah's aggressive attitude to Herat did not please the British government. Rawlinson returned to Bombay.

He was able in 1839 to publish a number of articles on his researches including an account of his journeys for the Royal Geographical Society. He was seeking a post preferably in Turkish Arabia, which would enable him to carry on his studies of ancient Persian and the cuneiform script. He was offered a post on Sir William Macnaughton's staff. Macnaughton was chief political officer of the army in Afghanistan In 1841 at the age of 30, Rawlinson went to Kandahar, the Western Capital of Afghanistan, as British consul or political agent. The situation was far from stable, Shah Soojah the British puppet had been installed in place of Dost Mohammed and had made various promises which he was unable or unwilling to keep. Herat rescued from the Persians with British help had become almost independent under Shah Kanran, now elderly with effective power in the hands of his ambitious and aggressive visier Yar Mohammed. Eventually the appearance of peace was established and by late 1842 Rawlinson was even able to persuade the populace to pay some taxes despite Shah Soojah having remitted them in total for a large proportion of the area.

In November 1842 disaster struck and the whole British effort in Afghanistan collapsed leading to a disastrous retreat. Rawlinson acted as a magistrate in Kandahar dispensing justice till just before sunset when it was his custom to ride his horse in the surroundings. For three days the pressure of business lasted till after dark preventing him from having his ride. At the end of the third day a fresh prisoner was brought in who had just assassinated Rawlinson's secretary. The man was a religious fanatic who had picked the lot which picked him for the assassination. He had been in the square waiting for Rawlinson without food or drink for three days at the end of which he attacked and killed the first available Englishman. He was executed by being fired from a cannon.

Meanwhile Kabul had fallen to the rebels. McNaughton had been killed and a military relief expedition had failed to get through because of snow in the passes. Sufder Jung, a son of Shah Soojah, defected to the rebel chief Atta Mohammed Khan and suported by the Dooranis produced a menacing situation. However a sortie lead by General Nott and accompanied by Major Rawlinson was successful leading to a defeat of the rebels and Sufder Jung and Atta Mohammed Khan had to seek refuge with the Dooranis. At this point General Nott decided to confront Mirza Ahmed in battle. He set out from Kandahar with most of the army leaving Rawlinson in charge of Kandahar. The rebels retreated before Nott who pursued them in apparent success. However the rebels having lead Nott some distance from Kandahar doubled back and infested the old town where they were joined by Saloo Khan with a thousand men. There were about eight or nine thousand rebels camped round Kandahar. Rawlinson sent three messengers to Nott asking him to return immediately. An elderly peasant approached the Herat Gate after closing time. Apologising for his lateness he nonetheless tried to persuade the gate keepers to admit him while busily unloading brushwood against the gate. Eventually he set light to the brushwood and fired the gate. The rebels pressed forward and even more when the gate collapsed outwards. However the soldiers on duty kept their posts and shot anyone who tried to come through the arch.

The Shahapoor Gate and the Kabul Gate were also attacked but the rebels failed to fire these. The rebels lost many men in the attack which had failed and lost confidence in Mirza Ahmed and nearly assassinated him. Rawlinson had success-fully defended Kandahar. Meanwhile supplies and money were running out, partly because Mirza Ahmed was collecting the taxes and also because General England bringing relief from Sind was reluctant to come through the Bolan and Khojuck passes. He was persuaded to do so when the Kandahar men, under Colonel Wymer, cleared the heights above the passes of rebels. Meanwhile the supposed puppet King Shah Soojar had written to the Dooranis asking them to continue attacking the army based at Kandahar. Mirza Ahmed and Mohammed Atta were still at large. General Nott wished to offer a reward for the capture of these two. Rawlinson advised against it for fear of reprisals against the British trapped in Kabul. He succeeded in persuading Nott. However both he and Nott were thinking in terms of a relief of Kabul and a restoration of friendly control. They were shocked when Lord Ellenbrough the Governor General ordered the Kandahar regiments to withdraw from Kandahar to Sukkur via Quetta. A successful skirmish with rebel troops and the evacuation of a subsidiary post were accomplished. Sufder Jung defected back to the British. Fresh order arrived from the Governor General giving Nott the option of withdrawing through the Khojuck Pass to Quetta or going via Ghuzni, Kabul, and Jellalabad. Nott chose the latter. He divided his forces sending part South to Quetta under General England. The other part left for Ghuzni. Rawlinson's political post having come to an end, he became Nott's aide de camp.

The entire British force evacuated Kandahar with no trouble on August 7th 1842. Soojah Jung had two sons, Timour and Sufder Jung. The latter was appointed governor of Kandahar and left in charge. Timour was taken with the evacuating army. Nott's group managed 160 miles before encountering any opposition. This happened at a place called Mookoor and the opponent was one Shumshooden Khan who after some success against troops guarding foragers, lost out after another skirmish. Nott advanced towards Ghuzni which was Shumshooden Khan's base. Just short of Ghuzni was a village called Rosa, which contained the tomb of Sulton Mahmoud of Ghuznii, which was alleged to be guarded by gates plundered from the temple at Somnaugh in India. Lord Ellenborough had given orders these were to be returned to Somnaugh so they were removed from Rosa. On the morning of the proposed attack on Ghuzni it was found the occupying rebels had fled and the town was deserted. The town walls were demolished and the town fired. The march to Kabul continued on 10th September. On the 14th at Mydan they heard that Akbar Khan had been defeated and General Pollock had gained a victory, giving him control of Kabul.. Nott continued fighting his way through, passed Urgundubeh on the 15th and was approaching Kabul on the 17th. It was at Urgundubeh that Rawlinson proposed himself as messenger to

General Pollock which was agreed and setting off in Afghan dress with Peshewar escort he did indeed contact General Pollock and returned with a letter from him on his views of the general situation. He returned to British India with Generals Nott and Pollock and their forces through Jugdullah, Jellalabad, The Khyber Pass and Attock, arriving at Ferozepoor on December 1st On arrival he was asked for accounts of his expenditure and while he had naturally collected all necessary receipts over three years and kept them, he had been obliged to send them with General England's forces. Unfortunately while sailing on the River Sutlej, the boat containing these documents caught fire destroying all Rawlinson's documentation. The military authorities accepted this fact but still demanded accounts. Rawlinson expected to be ruined but during the next six months managed to remember much of the detail and persuaded the providers of the original receipts to provide duplicates and considering how many of these were Kandaharis its speaks well of his reputation there. Most other political agents got a gong but not Rawlinson,. Representations were made and he was made a Commander of the Bath on the 22nd February 1844

He had intended to return to England but on a voyage from Allahabad to Calcutta, down the Ganges he met Lord Ellenborough who was sufficiently impressed to offer him the residency in Nepal or the post of Governor General's agent in Central India. Rawlinson declined both these posts for the inferior and took the less well paid post of political agent in Turkish Arabia which brought him to Baghdad in October 1843. He was there for five years and during that time transcribed the Persian inscription on Darius's mausoleum at Nakah I Rustam and deciphered the cuneiform as well. This opened to Western Scholarship the whole ancient world of Persia, Assyria and Babylon. The area round the twin rivers of the Tigris and the Euphrates was/ one of the chief regions in which our culture had its beginnings. The inscription on the crag at Behuistan is three hundred feet above the plain and the climb though not out of the way to an experienced mountaineer is difficult for the ordinary tourist. Rawlinson managed to finish the Persian and the median inscriptions and all the detached Babylonian epitaphs, The chief Babylonian inscription was out of reach without either a better cragsman or better apparatus. Darius's workman had carefully prepared the rock, cutting out weaker areas and inbedding harder stone with lead, and then varnishing the whole. This varnish enabled some of the letters to be read which might otherwise have disintegrated. On the way back to Baghdad via Zagros and the Diyelah River he transcribed the Sassanian inscription of Pai Kuli. While he was in Baghdad he had a pet Mongoose which controlled snakes and vermin, a tame leopard called Fahad which he eventually presented to a zoo in Bristol, but used to visit to the animals delight and a tame lion. Sir Henry Layard was excavating upstream from Baghdad but all his discoveries passed through Rawlinson's hands. In 1846 the two met Layard had travelled down from Mosul by steamer and they found much to discuss and much to admire in each other. He saw much of what Layard produced and did a transcription of the Black Obelisk at Nimrud. He then realised that the Assyrian script and the Babylonian script wre very similar and that if it were possible to transcribe the full text of the hitherto inaccessible Babylonian inscription at Behuistan then a means of translating the script, because of the trilingual nature of Behuistan, might appear. So he set off with ladders and ropes and the assistance of nimble footed goatherds. One in particular a Kurdish youth, managed to get above the inscription and driving in a peg and attaching a rope endeavoured to abseil down to it but was defeated by the projection of the rock. However the lad found another way up, drove in a second peg with rope attached, and made a seat attached to the two ropes level with the inscription and took paper mache impressions till the whole was recovered.

In 1849 he returned to England on two years leave of absence. He was made a Fellow of the Royal Society in 1850 for "the discovery of the key to ancient Persian, Babylonian and Assyrian in cuneiform" In 1851 he was promoted to Lt Colonel and published his text of the Behuistan inscription. He returned as Lt Col Rawlinson to Baghdad in 1851 and stayed a further five years, continuing his investigations. He received assistance from the British Museum to continue the excavations started by Sir Henry Layard and made many interesting and useful discoveries. Among them was the marble inscription describing the siege of Lachish by Sennacherib's forces, It was in Sennacherib's palace, Koynaye and was in a very bad condition. It was removed by Rawlinson and Hormazrd Rassam and restored by Rawlinson. It is now in a basement gallery of the British Museum. There was a cylinder of a King of Sidiken, a grandson of a Shalmaneser and contempory of Asher-izar-pal. A lengthy inscription of Nebuchadusur, King of Babylon and son of Nabopalusor.. His assistant Mr Loftus discovered that the River Karkah near Susa had had two separate branches in ancient time, the Eulaesir to the East and the Choasfo to the West. He had been wishing to return to England for some time but had been prevailed upon to stay. However in early 1855 he broke a collar bone while hunting wild boar. He returned to England in May 1855 and retired on full pay October 1855. He was made a director of the East India Co. and also made a Knight of the Bath. On the transfer of the government of India from the East India Co to the Crown he became a member of the first India Council a post he held until appointed Her Majesty's Envoy and Minister Plenipotentiary to the Shah of Persia in approximately 1859. The Shah welcomed him as an old friend, but he realized the British position in Persia was weakening and that of the Russians growing. He resigned after the direction of the consulate was changed from the India Office to the Foreign Office.which change took place almost as soon as he arrived in Tehran. He had no great opinion of the Foreign Office's grasp of affairs in the Near East or the approaches to India or the menace provided by the Russian Empire. He left Tehran finally on the 18th May 1860. . He had become MP for Reigate in 1857 resigning in 1858 to take up the post of envoy to the Shah. He became MP for Frome from 1865-1868. He seconded the MP for Poole (his brother in law Henry Danby Seymour) in his resolution that an army be sent into Abyssinia to rescue the consul and 50 British subjects all held in prison in appalling conditions by the Emperor Theodore. This was passed and the enterprise successfully carried out. He was appointed to the Council for India in 1868 necessitating his resig-

nation from parliament. He remained a member of the council till his death.. He was an advocate of a forward policy in Afghanistan and was suspicious of Russian intentions accurately predicting that they would absorb Khohan, Bokhara and Khive (they are now part of Uzbek-istan). He was made a baronet in 1891. The title survives to the present day. In 1862 at St George's Hanover Square he married Louise Caroline Harcourt Seymour daughter of Henry Seymour. The ceremony was taken by his brother Revd George Rawlinson They had two sons Henry Seymour 1864, and Alfred 1867-1934, who became the 3rd baronet.

Sir Henry Creswick Rawlinson Bt

Henry Seymour Rawlinson Lord Rawlinson 1864-1925

Henry was the eldest son of Sir Henry Creswick Rawlinson. He was trained at Sandhurst, served under Kitchener at Omdurman. He served in the 2nd Boer War and was involved in the battle of Rooiwal. He was then was appointed commandant of the Army Staff College which he modernized thoroughly. In the First World War he was the officer commanding the 4th Division, was virtually in charge of the Battle of the Somme and later in 1918 of the Battle of Amiens which was a British victory. He helped the breakthrough of the Hindenberg Line. In 1920 he was Commander in Chief for India. He was promoted to General and was made a baron for his services. He was married to Meredith Kennard but they had no children so the peerage died with him and the baronetcy passed to his brother Alfred.

Revd Professor George Rawlinson 1812-1902

George was the third son of Abraham Tysack Rawlinson. He was a student at Trinity College Oxford. He played cricket for the university. After graduating he became a fellow of Exeter College in 1840 and was fellow and tutor, 1842-46. He had been ordained in 1841 and in 1846 he went as curate to the village of Merton till 1847. He was the Bampton Lecturer in 1859 and from 1861-69 he was Camden Professor of Ancient History at Oxford.. In 1872 he was appointed Rector of All Hallows Lombard St in the City of London. He published a translation of Herodotus in collaboration with his brother and Sir John Gardner Wilkinson, "The Five Great Monarchies of the Ancient Eastern World" " The Sixth Great Oriental Monarchy (Parthian)" " The Seventh Great Oriental Monarchy (Sassanian)"," Manual of Ancient History", "Historical Illustratiions of the Old Testament", " The Origin of Nations ", History of Ancient Egypt", " Egypt and Babylon", "Histoiry of Phoenecia" " Parthia", "Memoir of Sir H C Rawlinson" and " The Historical Evidences of the Truth of the Scriptures Stated Anew" . In 1846 he married Louisa Chermside

Henry Lindow Rawlinson born 1776 later Henry Lindow Lindow

Henry was the second son of Henry Rawlinson MP for Liverpool. He inherited an estate in St Vincent either from his Aunt Abigail or her husband William Lindow on condition that he took the name Lindow

Thomas Hutton Rawlinson 1712-69

Fifth son of Abraham Rawlinson of Lancaster 1636-1737. He was a Quaker and a slave trader as well as a West India merchant. He worked with his brother Abraham 1709-80. They imported mahogany for Gillows, the furniture company. In 1739 he was the firm's representative in Barbados. In 1741 the major part of the cargo for the return trip from the West Indies were goods he had acquired. He married Mary Dilworth daughter of John Dilworth another slave trader, and grandson of Thomas Satterthwaite of Hawkshead. There are portraits of him and his wife by Romney in Lancaster museum. They had the following children; Sarah wife of John Chorley (son of Alexander and Rebecca Chorley of Rainford another slaver), Elizabeth wife of Isaac Ford, Abraham, Lydia 1738-98, Thomas Hutton, Dilworth, John and William. He was a freeman of the City of Lancaster as was his son Thomas Hutton. He and his brother owned the following ships "Molly" 1743, "Ellen" 1746, "Jane" 1746 "Recovery" 1746 and "Industry" 1744-1752.

He endowed the Friends School in Lancaster. He was called Captain Rawlinson so presumably he had actually captained a ship at least once rather than employing other people to make the voyages.

Thomas Hutton Rawlinson slave trader

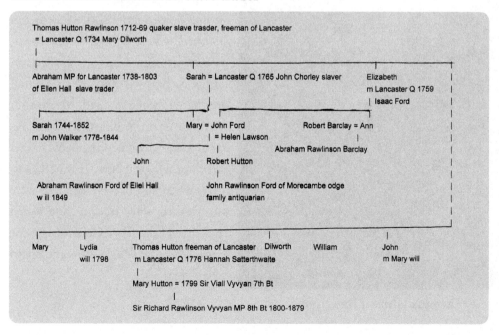

The brothers did have agents permanently resident in the West Indies and would have shares in plantations and therefore own slaves. At this period slaving was a matter of buying slaves from African slave dealers rather than landing a party and kidnapping people. It is possible that Sir John Hawkins tried that back in Queen Elizabeth's time and found it unsatisfactory. The difficulty was the prevalence of disease.

It is not easy to ascertain when the Rawlinsons began to be involved in the slave trade, which began to get going after the restoration of the monarchy in 1662. In 1772 the Mansfield judgment was handed down which meant that slavery was held to be illegal in the United Kingdom. People like John Chance, who was presumably brought over as a slave of William Lindow became a servant. There were possibly similar people in the Rawlinson households. An adult black man called Isaac Rawlinson was baptised at St Mary Lancaster. In 1808 slave trading per se was abolished. So the grandchildren of Abraham and Thomas Hutton Rawlinson lived through to a time when slave trading was abolished. It was another generation before owner-

ship of slaves overseas was made illegal in 1833. People like Abraham Tyzack Rawlinson drew income from slave estates but were not actively involved in their management. After 1833 several descendents of the Rawlinson brothers were among those compensated. Thomas Hutton Rawlinson states in his will that he co-owned an estate in Grenada with his brother Abraham and William Lindow. As far as I know none of the Rawlinsons were in the Royal Navy from 1833 to 1900 when part of their activities were suppressing slave trading. He was a member of the Port Commision for Lancaster from 1665-1668 and again 1761- 1765

Thomas Hutton Rawlinson

Abraham Rawlinson MP 1738-1803

Abraham was son of Thomas Hutton Rawlinson. He took over his father's business and refounded it in 1756 as Abraham Rawlinson Jnr. He. Mary Rawlinson and Lydia Rawlinson each had a one sixth share. He actually went on one slave trading voyage himself. In 1756 eight out of seventeen vessels trading from Lancaster to the West Indies belonged to the Rawlinsons. They traded in slaves and mahogany. The Rawlinsons were suppliers to Gillows the furniture makers. He was an MP for Lancaster, 1780-1790. He was baptized, at St Mary Lancaster on Lady Day 1780. This would have enabled him to sit in parliamentand was probably the motive for the baptism.

He was a vigorous and persistent opponent of the abolition of slavery. In 1783 and 1785 he voted for parliamentary reform. He built Ellel Hall near Lancaster. He, too, was painted by Romney. I include a quote from his letter book written by him in 1792 "The people of England want to lower the price of sugar and yet continue to present petitions from all quarters to parliament to procure the abolition of the slave trade. Many have left off the use of sugar for the purpose of putting an end to the slave trade. If this custom become prevalent of eating and using nothing touched by slaves we may soon expect to see people in the state of their first nature. Naked in the fields feeding like Nebuchadnezzer on grass. What wonder their philanthropy and enthusiasm will produce is unknown" At the time it was thought enthusiasm was a very bad thing. John Wesley was accused of it.

Abraham was a freeman of the City of Lancaster. He married Anne, daughter of Robert and Elizabeth Dodgson of Sherburn in 1766. They had no children. He and his brother John were removed from membership of the Quakers for carrying arms on their ships and seizing the property of others. This was the same meeting as heard there Uncle Abraham and Cousin Thomas's angry refutationof the same charge.

John Rawlinson Ford has a number of stories handed down about members of the family. There is one about an Abraham Rawlinson who I presume is this one as the one most closely related to Ford. "Abraham as a teenager found the Quaker meeting rather boring, Ford states the service had evolved to the form known as the Quaker Silence, very different from the heady preaching of George Fox. In order to sustain the tedium young Abraham had got into the habit of taking a quantity of gingerbread in with him. One day he stood up holding a piece of gingerbread in his hand and offered it as a reward for the first person to speak. He was rebuked by one of the elders.

John Rawlinson,1741-1799, merchant Lancaster

Brother of the preceeding

In 1785 Abraham & John Rawlinson were the second largest exporters of cloth, (presumably Lancashire, possibly Lancaster), they also exported paper and hams. Abraham's partner John was his younger brother. In the 1790s it seems to be John who took a leading role The letter books donated by John Rawlinson Ford, a descendant of their sister Elizabeth's show John writing to the various agents in the islands talking mainly about coffee, sugar and cocoa and how they are to be purchased. Their Voyage Book lists ships and captains and the cargo of the ships going out from Lancaster. John Rawlinson Ford's papers were donated to Lancaster Museum and are now in the Lancashire County Archives at Preston. John was Married at Shotton Quakers in 1766 at the same ceremony as his brother Abraham. John's wife was Mary Heighington daughter of John and Anne Heighington merchant Durham. Theyhad two sons Thomas Hutton Rawlinson 1769-1787 and John Rawlinson 1770-1772. All six parents were there with John Rawlinson Jnr a son of their Uncle Abraham and an Isaac Rawlinson Jr. John's grandfather Abraham had a son Isaaac who had married at the Church of England and had had several children including an Isaac who could be the witness.

Sir Richard Rawlinson Vivyan of Trelowran Cornwall 8th Bt 1800-1879 MP FRS

He was the son of Sir Vyell Vivyan, by Mary only child of Thomas Hutton Rawlinson Jnr son of Thomas Hutton Rawlinson Snr. Her mother was Hannah Satterthwaite who belonged to another Lancaster slaving family originating from Hawkshead.

He was MP successively for Okehampton, Bristol and Helston. He opposed the Emancipation and Reform Bills. He was a scientist but supported Lamarcks theory of evolution. He voted for the resolution that brought down the Wellington administration. He was opposed to free trade.

RAWLINSON OF GRAY'S INN, HENDON AND GILTHWAITERIGGE

John Rawlinson of Grays Inn barrister 1629-99

John was the second son of William Rawlinson the militia captain as is clear from correspondence he left behind, (now in Lancaster Archives) and his own will. As well as his London house, John had land at Whittington alias Newton in Lancashire and also in Rusland, Force Forge and Boldrae Moss. His executor was his brother Sir William who was also a trustee along with John Sharp, Archbishop of York (William's brother in law) . He was admitted to Grays Inn in 1689 described as the brother of Sir William Rawlinson who was his younger brother. On 12th February 1688 John wrote a letter from the office of the Master of the Rolls to his brother Thomas at Graythwaite reporting that the Princess of Orange had arrived safely in Whitehall and that, the Prince and she looked to every house to proclaim them King and Queen. He held the office of Secretary to the Master of the Rolls in 1688

John was baptised at Hawkshead having been born at Graythwaite. He was of Furnival's Inn 1676, barrister at law of Grays Inn having entered Gray's Inn in 1689.He made his will in 1698 and this was in effect proved in 1700. However, before probate it had been challenged and subjected to review, the substance of the review was called a sentence. He was Secretary to Master of the Rolls 1688,

He had acquired Rusland Hall under a deed of settlement of 1686 and afterwards purchased Whittington Hall. He appears in the Satterthwaite Asessments in 1685 and 1693. He left Whittington Hall to whichever son of his nephew William, son of his brother Thomas, should adhere to the Church of England, within seven years of his death. No one came forward in the time allowed. In fact his great nephew Thomas adhered to the Church of England in 1733 having been brought up a Quaker and was of Whittington Hall and Invergarry. Clearly John disapproved the

Quaker connection deriving from his brother's conversion. Apart from Thomas of Invergarry the rest stuck with the Quakers at least until John Job's birth in 1798.

John Rawlinson of Hullater of the Grizadale Branch acted as local agent in Furness for John Rawlinson of the Rolls Inn. They consistantly addressed each other as "Cousin" despite the difference of status, wealth and branch.

Hullater (a fairly modern house) lies to the left of the picture just below the hill locally called "The Camel's Back).

William Rawlinson MP a commissioner of the Great Seal, Father of the House of Commons

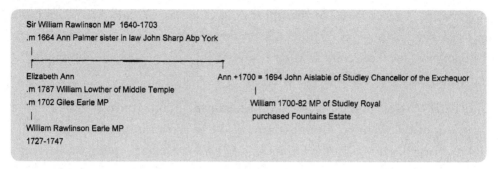

```
Sir William Rawlinson MP  1640-1703
.m 1664 Ann Palmer sister in law John Sharp Abp York

  |
  |----------------------------------------------|
Elizabeth Ann                                    Ann +1700 = 1694 John Aislabie of Studley Chancellor of the Exchequor
.m 1787 William Lowther of Middle Temple           |
.m 1702 Giles Earle MP                           William 1700-82 MP of Studley Royal
  |                                                 purchased Fountains Estate
William Rawlinson Earle MP
1727-1747
```

Sir William Rawlinson 1640-1703

The Victoria County History says William was the second son of William Rawlinson the militia captain. Actually he was the third son behind Thomas who became a Quaker and John b 1629 who was a lawyer of Grays Inn who left behind correspondence now in Lancaster archives clearly identifying him as a son of the militia captain. William was of Gray's Inn in 1665 when he bought land at Roosecote from Thomas Hutton of Pooleton; the money was to be paid over at Gilthwaitrigge. In 1660 he had paid £1200 for Gilthwaitrigge and its water cornmill,moss and turbary in Brigsteer to Edward Turner of Kirkby Kendall and his son Thomas Turner. In 1668 he assigned the rents and receipts of the messuage and tenement of Gilthwaitrigge to his father. In 1695 he leased Gilthwaitrigge for a year to Rowland Scales, then in occupation. The property had previously been occupied by Thomas Sleddall, deceased, his son Robert Sleddall and John Mitchell.. In 1694 and 1695 he had been giving legal advice to Sir Daniel Fleming of Rydal Westmorland. In 1703 William's widow sold Gilthwaitrigge to William Rawlinson of Graythwaite.

William was serjent at law, one of the commissioners of the great seal 1688-93, and MP for Hendon and was an MP long enough to become Father of the House of Commons. He was a supporter of the Glorious Revolution that brought William III and Mary II to the throne. His wife was Anne Palmer of Winthorp in Lincolnshire. For a time he lived in Chancery Lane. In 1667 his wife's sister Elizabeth married John Sharp the future Archbishop of York who lived with them for four years. He was buried at Hendon. He had two daughters Elizabeth wife of William Lowther and then Giles Earle MP, who she married in 1702 and Ann wife of John Aislabie of Studley Royal whom she married in 1694. The friendship with the Sharp family evidently continued as Elizabeth Prowse and her husband, of Wicken Park Northamptonshire called on Mr and Mrs Giles Earle on their way north to visit Elizabeth's brother, Archdeacon Sharp of Hartburn. William's widow, his second wife Jane Nosworthy, was buried at Ealing in 1712 and endowed a girls school.

Giles Earle 1678-1758 was MP for Chippenham and Malmesbury. He was a strong supporter of the Walpole administration and had served in the army under the Duke of Argyll. He was in the Commons 1715-47. He had a rather coarse wit . His son William Rawlinson Earle 1702-1774 was also MP for various seats being in the Commons 1727-68. He was also a supporter of Walpole but managed to survive his fall.

John Aislabie 1670-1742 was born in York and eventually inherited the Studley Royal Estate. His mother had been a Mallory. He was MP for Ripon in 1695 and later for Northallerton and again for Ripon. Initially he was supposedly a Tory but finished up as Chancellor of the Exchequer in a Whig administration. He steered the South Sea Company bill through the Commons in 1719 . When it crashed in 1720 it was discovered he had taken an unofficial commission of £20,000. He was prosecuted and imprisoned in the Tower. After his release he returned to Studley. He had married Ann in 1694 and they had one son William, and three daughters. Ann died in a fire at their house in Red Lion Square London along with one of the daughters. He was an early landscape gardener and the elegant water garden and associated temples and statuary are his. He was responsible for laying them out to be visible from terraces on higher ground. Each waterfall is engineered to fall at a different note. His son William added the ruins of Fountains Abbey to the garden. In 1717 John married Judith Vernon but had no further children. Ann' s relationship to Archbishop Sharpe helped Aislabie's career to get off the ground.

THE REPROBATES derived from letters held at Barrow and Preston

Ebenezer Rawlinson 1708-1760

Ebenezer was a son of William Rawlinson of Graythwaite by his second wife Mary Willison, widow of Isaac Willison, and daughter of Robert Benson of Penrith grocer,. In 1731 he is a subscriber to a book of poems published by his cousin Isaac Thompson of Newcastle. He took five copies. He is preceded in the list by Mr Isaac Rawlinson who also took five copies, this must be his uncle as his brother Isaac died in infancy. Mr Abraham Rawlinson Jnr follows him in the list and took two copies, he will be Ebenezer's nephew. In 1734 he was sued by his elder brother, Thomas along with his other brothers. Thomas claimed he had a right to inherit Graythwaite contrary to the provisions of their father's will. There was in 1734 a letter from Jo Benson (his mother's brother) to Job Rawlinson (his half brother) of Graythwaite about Ebenezer's unsatisfactory financial affairs. A letter from Job states that his father William will not leave Ebenezer in Bergen, but now he has seen his faults will settle his debts. On Christmas Day 1736 Ebenezer was baptized at Kendal thus leaving the Quakers for the Church of England. In 1747 Ebenezer was living at Dent in Yorkshire and married Elizabeth Stephenson of Newby Bridge at Cartmel in that year. In Captain Thomas Ollivant's will of 1747 he is left an annuity of £15 per annum. He commutes this to £150 cash by agreement with Thomas Benson of Carlisle an executor of the will in 1751. In 1758 he petitioned for payment of a debt for supplying goods outstanding by Rowland Taylor of Kendal currently a prisoner in the Marshalsea. He died at Castleton Malew Parish in the Isle Of Man in 1760 when a resident of Yorkshire. In the Bateman Letters at Birmingham University it is stated he often wrote asking for money clsaiming on one occasion to be buying a ship and on another to have been robbed on the moor.

Adam

In a letter of 1688(1698) from Isaac Rawlinson at the six clerks office to William Rawlinson he states:" Cousin Adam left a week ago. He is grossly impure if the report I hear is true and this may be the reason for his going away". He had met with Cousin James Pearson and had missed Cousin Thomas Chatburn

Isaac will be the youngest son of Thomas Rawlinson who became a Quaker. He was born in 1680. He was at school in Penketh in 1697 and later stayed with Henry Gouldney in London, presumably training for a life as a merchant. Pearson and Chatburn are the sons of two Rawlinson sisters who were Aunts of Isaac's . Chatburn was at the six clerks office and both acted as London agents for other members of the family. Who Adam is is a mystery. Another Aunt of Isaac's married an Adam Storrs and there were Adams in the Gouldney family.

Isaac

William Rawlinson of Knaresbrough and Rusland writing to his wife Mally from London in 1713 warns her against Isaac who, he says has returned from America where he lived a dissolute and promiscuous life including sexual relations with blacks. This Isaac has managed to obtain money from Brother Oldner in Newcastle. William is afraid that Isaac wlll arrive at Graythwaite before he returns himself. He describes Isaac as a most wicked person.

Mally Rawlinson is the daughter of Robert Benson a grocer of Penrith. William refers to brother Benson as being in London who is presumably her brother John. Quakers tended to refer to fellow quakers as brother but in this case George Oldner had married Alice Benson, Mally's sister.

The only Isaac Rawlinson who would be of the right age is the correspondent writing about Adam, above. There was an Isaac born and buried 1701 a son of William and Mally and an Isaac born in 1704 to Abraham Rawlinson and wife who later moved to Caton who would be too young . Mally Rawlinson had had a son Isaac by her first marriage to Isaac Willison.

APPENDIX I
Other Rawlinson Families

There are other people called Rawlinson in Furness and elsewhere. Joseph Rawlinson who owned some of the iron ore mines in Dalton parish and was an early ship builder in Barrow in Furness is commemorated in street names in both Barrow and Dalton. He soon sold out his ship building interest to Fishers. There was a family of Rawlinsons at Beckside in Cartmel who produced a wife for Princess Alexandra's son James Ogilvie. In neither case is there any known connection.

Peter Rawlinson was solicitor general in Mrs Thatcher's government and was created Lord Rawlinson of Ewell.

His father Arthur Rawlinson, after a military career, turned to film and television directing and produced a series on Samuel Pepys which featured Daniel Rawlinson of the Mitre, Fenchurch St, London who is one of the Grisedale Rawlinsons. The publicity material claimed that Daniel Rawlinson was a great grandfather of Arthur Rawlinson. Now in producing publicity material of this sort a man is not on oath, but it has to be said that it isn't true. Daniel had sons, grandsons, great grandsons but there is no sign that he has male line descendents into the twentieth century. Arthur Rawlinson's antecedents are in Hampshire. His father and grandfather were both called Thomas. His great grandfather was John Rawlinson, 1777-1847 of Combe Hampshire who purchased New Place Alresford also Hampshire one of whose sons was Sir Christopher Rawlinson, Chief Justice of Madras. John's father was another John who was baptized in Hackney in 1747 became a physician at St Thomas's and retired to Combe and died in1798. This John's parents were Christopher Rawlinson 1703-75 of Bowling Green House near Chatham Place London and Combe Hampshire by his wife Margaret Rawlinson whom he married at Hackney in 1729. Christopher was baptized in1703 at Loughton Essex. He was the son of another Christopher who was buried in Hackney in 1731. Further back is a little obscure. However John Rawlinson of Combe House

97

Alresford Hampshire, citizen and haberdasher of London and deputy sherriff of Southampton who married Eleanor Whistler. He died in 1689 His son John died in 1725 and evidently had no surviving children. In his will he makes provision for his wife Ann and his mother, who had remarried and had become Eleanor Joy.

He then left money to a) John Rawlinson apothecary of Hackney. He was still alive in 1750 and had married in 1706 Elizabeth Garbrand and had a daughter Margaret who might be the same as the one married at Hackney in 1729.

And b) to the children of Christopher Rawlinson of Ingram Grange Coxwold Yorks including said Christopher's sons Christopher and John which last Christopher may be the one buried at Hackney in 1739.

Both the earlier and later Rawlinsons owned property in the same places. Arthur Rawlinson's claim of kinship to Daniel Rawlinson of the Mitre may have some substance as there is a John Rawlinson born at Haverthwaite who could be the John Rawlinson buried at Combe in 1680, However, there is no evidence for this and rests solely on Arthur's doubtful claim. Daniel Rawlinson's dates were 1616-79. He did have a son John, b 1648 vintner of London who made a will in 1689, proved 1696, leaving everything to his sister Margaret Honour and is therefore not the same person as John Rawlinson, haberdasher who married Eleanor Whistler. However when John Rawlinson, the haberdasher died his children were minors so his estate was examined by the court of orphans which saw what assets were available including debts inward and outward This showed both Curwen Rawlinson MP of Cark and Mr William Rawlinson (presumably MP for Hendon) both belong to the Greenhead Graythwaite family owing money to John Rawlinson, having been customers of his.

APPENDIX II

The grant by letters patent to the Whitmore brothers

Sir William Whitmore was a London merchant trading in Spanish textiles, Sir George Whitmore was Lord Mayor of London, the Patent Roll for 11th year of James I part 7 number 23 grants them the following :-

1) Manor and Bailliewick of Colton

2) meadow and three acres demesne at Colton

3) land and tenement in Sales and Crake 58/12

4) land and tenement in Bouth £4/7/6

5) land and tenement in Heybrig and Kirkthwaite 26/2

6) land and tenement in Oxen Park 40/7

7) land and tenement in Bandrighead and Abbots Park

8) land and tenement in Icornthwaite 26/-

9) All the results of the Greenwood in Colton

10)- All the perquisites of the Manor of Colton £24/4/5 excluding 54/6 bloomsmithy rents to the bailiff of Hawkshead Manor

11) All the manor and bailliewick of Haverthwaite £4/17/8

12) Haverthwaite fishings presently occupied by Christopher Preston receiver of Furness £3/6/3

13) Manor of Finsthwaite interior and exterior

14) Stott Park and Rusland and results from Greenwood therein

15) Manor of Satterthwaite

16) land in Grizedale and Dale Park

Excluding advowsons and right of patronage, my true and lawfull attornies Miles Dodding of Conishead and Edmund Sawyer of London.

APPENDIX III

London Evening Post no 8452
Thursday Dec 14th - Saturday December 16th 1749

Extract of letter from Antigua 6 September 1749

Thomas Clarkson, late mate of a snow of Liverpool (wherein Thomas Rawlinson was late commander), Thomas Knowles boatswain, John Blunditt labourer on board said vessell give following account. They sailed from Liverpool 21st October 1748 with a cargo of dry goods bound for the Coast of Africa arrived Bonane on the windward coast 5th December, embarked 120 negroe slave but lost 15 by disease. Captain Rawlinson and the doctor were sick there, but that all the whites on board, 13 in number, took all necessary precautions to secure the slaves, putting them in irons and locking them down the hatches.

On June 11[th,] while riding at anchor, the slaves rose against them, several of whom had by some means got off their irons and laid hold of great billets of wood with which they did much mischief. The crew defended themselves, and kept the deck two hours before being overpowered, one of them killed and all the rest wounded, they were obliged to retreat to the cabin which all but the carpenter did (although often summoned) and, trusting to the mercy of the Negroes, he was cut to pieces upon deck. The rest kept possession till the afternoon of the next day when the Negroes ripped up the quarter deck and then five of the crew jumped overboard thinking to reach Captain Rawlinson who had put off with three armed canoes, though in vain, to suppress the insurrection but the Negroes having got to the

100

fire arms shot the five people in the sea while they were swimming. Thus, being obliged to abandon the cabin they fled to the last resort the powder room where they received frequent messages from the negroes above requiring them to surrender but they being resolute and assured them that they would blow up the rest of the vessel. The Negroes sent no more but ran the snow aground, getting on shore themselves, the vessel bulged and the natives plundered her of everything worth taking away, even the wearing apparel of the remainder of the crew. Before their departure Captain Rawlinson as was **unlegised** through grief for the ill success of the voyage not withstanding the care which had been taken to render it otherwise. Slaves being a valued commodity in the West Indies.

unlegised I transcribed this from a cutting from the Evening Post kept in the Rawlinson manuscripts by hand and in pencil. My handwriting is not good and unlegised is the best I could make of this word when I came to type up my notes. I take it to mean that Rawlinson still suffering from the effects of his illness and further shocked by the disaster which had overcome him, the loss of his ship, the deaths of his crew, the loss of his investment which possibly represented his whole fortune, gave up the ghost and died.

APPENDIX IV
Rawlinson entries in Subsidy Rolls for Lonsdale

1547
Dalton in Furness
John Renldson
Robert Rawlinson

Colton
William Rawlinson
John Rawlinson Hullater
Edward Rawlinson Crakeside

Hawkshead
Richard Rawlinson

1581
Dalton in Furness
Leonard Rawlinson

1598
Colton
John Rawlinson
John Rawlinson bailiff

Dalton in Furness
Leonard Rawlinson

Hawkshead
Robert Rawlinson

1629
Dalton in Furness
John Rawlinson in goods

1641
Dalton in Furness
Robert Rawlinson gt
Leonard Rawlinson

Hearth Tax 1663
Holker
Robert Rawlinson

The original Greenhead Farm has been extensively modernised in recent years. It consisted of two stories with the humans living upstairs and the animals below, the heat from the animals helped keep the humans warm. Two substantial wings have been added at either end. The piece in the middle represents the original building. Graythwaite is the modern spelling but Graithwaite appears in many early documents. I use Graythwaite apart from the tabular pedigrees where Graithwaite may be used.

Greenhead Farm Colton

LONG PEDIGREE OF RAWLINSON OF GREENHEAD, GRAYTHWAITE, LANCASTER, ETC

Symbols used here and in tabular pedigrees

fl flourished ie alive

= married

m married

unm unmarried

b = born

c = baptized

+ = died

ob = died

bur = buried

dsp = died without children

gt = gentleman

16 James 1 = 16th year of King James 1st

JP = Justice of the Peace

MI = memorial inscription

dau = daughters

Bp = Bishop

2 D = 2nd Duke

Wd = Westmorland

Sw = Swarthmoor

M/C = Manchester

Lpl = Liverpool

Kn = Knaesbrough

Nlln = Northallerton

Boyd Percival = Boyd's lists and indexes

Bt = Baronet

And = Andrew

ca = about

Sq = Square

RN = Royal Navy

16 4 1622 = 16th April 1622

s = son of

a = before (ante)

p 1678 = after 1678

Q = ceremony at Quaker Meeting

C/E = Church of England

+ 1737 (48) = died 1737 aged 48

DL = Doctor of Laws

Mch = March

16 in 51 = aged 16 in 1851 (census)

town 91 = living in town in 1891

fff = and following years

adm = administration

Gp Capt = Group Captain

+ 22 11` 19xx = died sometime after 22nd November 1900

ex Malvern = went to Malvern School

TCC = Trinity College Cambridge

AuL = Ashton under Lyne

otp = of this parish

Lic = license to get married

Rawlinson of Greenhead

Robert Rawlinson of Greenhead Gill and Colton Mill in Colton fl 1484

John

William fl\Henry VIII

= 1509 daughter of Robert Benson of Low Wray and Skelwith

    John of Greenhead b 1525

    = Daughter of Myles Sawrey of Graythwaite

        William 1541 -1607 rebuilt Colton Church

        will 1607 of Greenhead

        = Margaret daughter William Pennington of Colton

            John of the Riddings = Avis

            William will 1619/20 purchased land and property in

            Greenhead from Christopher Sandes (spelling in source) of Bouth gt, Anthony Sawrey of Plumpton gt and Thomas Rawlinson of Grisedale gt 16 James I

            = 1610 Margaret dau Walter Curwen of Mireside

                        Cartmel

                Robert of Greenhead, Mireside, Cark Hall &

                Buck Hall Oxen b 1610, entered Gray's Inn 1634, JP

                Vice Chancellor of Chester

                cousin to Ann Fuller of Roehampton

                Capt William of Bucknell Hall Oxon

                leased Bucknell Manor Ho 1638 from Francis Ewer

                + 1643 MI Bucknell Church

                      William of Poultny ln London

                      = dau James Mossley

                Margaret = William Moore of Rowell

                Elizabeth

                = Cartmel 1632 John Swainson of Cartmel Fell

                      will 1638

              Ann

= Cartmel 1642 George Hutton of Thorpinsty

William

Agnes

Mary

daughter = Nicholas Singleton fl 1634

Francis

Adam fishmonger London, will 1625/30 of St Nicholas Cole
Abbey buried St Nicholas Cole Abbey 1630

= St Matthew, Friday Street 1622 Ellen Wheeler

daughter William Wheeler goldsmith

Eleanor + St Matthew Friday Street 1635

Ann + St Matthew Friday Street 1637

Margaret

Robert of Colton

Alice

Mary

Margarer

Thomas

William of Tottlebank claimed Force Smithy 1549

= Katherine dau of Myles Sawrey of Graythwaite and widow of
John Sawrey

Rawlinson of Cark

Robert Rawlinson of Greenhead, Mireside, Cark Hall and Buck Hall Oxon
b 1610, entered Gray's Inn 1634 JP Vice Chancellor of Chester
= 1639 Jane b 1620 dau Thomas Wilson of Heversham Hall + Hampsfield 1685
Curwen c Cartmel 1641 b Nether Cark, of Mireside and Cark Hall MP +1689
bought Holm Park
= St Andrew Holborn 1671 Elizabeth dau Nicholas Monk Bp Hereford and
niece George Monk D of Albemarle

Monk b 1671 of Gray's Inn 1692 bur Cartmel 1692 when of Cark

Christopher 1677-1733 published Saxon version of Boethius's
"Consolation of Philosophy

heir to cousin 2 D Albemarle but died too soon

will 1733 when of St Giles in the Fields

Elizabeth 1643

Edward c Colton 1644 fr Mr b Greenhead

Ann 1645

= (Boyd 1661) Christopher Crackenthorp of Newbiggin Wd 1630-69

    Ann

    Deborah

    Richard of Newbiggen ? Of Fetter Lane, Chiswick 1731

    = (Boyd 1690) Deborah Mottram

        Mottram of Newbiggi + unm

        Henry + infant

        Deborah + unm

        Ann = Burton in Kendal 1721 Dr Adam Askew of

                          Newcastle on Tyne

        Robert

        Christopher in 6 clerks office

        = Elizabeth dau S Wm Glynn Bt of Broad Lane, Flint

Dr George Bynard physician in Bristol

William c Cartmel 1647 student, St John's, Cambridge

Mary dsp 1768 = Charles Blake staymaker St Paul's Covent Garden

Catherine c Cartmel 1654

= Cartmel 1676 Roger Moore of Middleton KL sergeant at law

    Ann marriage bond 1716 when of Middleton + 1760 dsp

    = Revd William Aylmer of Warton 1714-34

    Catherine = 1704 Clement Rigge of Hawkshead

        Jane c Hawkshead 1706

        = St And by the Wardrobe 1767 Edward Moore of Stockwell

            Roger

        William c Hawkshead 1710

        Roger 1716 -45 b Keenground Hawkshead

        = 1736 Mary Fletcher 1720-1808

Fletcher 1741-1829 of Northallerton

= Ealing 1782 Susan Grey Sanders

John c Hawkshead 1718

Ellen 1656

Dorothy 1660

Jane 1662

Rawlinson of Cark II

Roger Rigg 1716-45 Keenground Hawkshead

= 1736 Mary Fletcher 1720-1808

Fletcher Rigg 1741 -1829 of Northallerton

= Ealing 1782 Susan Gray Sanders

Grey Fletcher Rigge c Nlln 1783 of West Broughton Hall

= 1803 Mary Moore of Stockwell a cousin

Henry Fletcher 1809 High Sherriff of West Broughton Hall

= Cartmel 1827 Rosetta dau James Matchell of Newby Bridge

Gray b ca 1857

Rosetta Ella b ca 1865

= St George Hanover Sq 1889 William Miller Rawlinson

= St Pancras 1903 George Rathbone musician

Captain Charles Gray RN will 1887 = Ellen Stockwell

Mary c Nlln 1784 = Francis Bedingfield of Ditchingham

Ann = St Paul Covent Garden John Hays of Kirkby in Westmorland

Ann = Revd Thomas Skelland

Lucy = 3rd Earl of Wiltshire

Rawlinson of Tottlebank

William Rawlinson of Tottlebank claimed Force Smithy 1549

= Katherine dau Miles Sawrey of Graythwaite and widow of John Sawrey +1547

Thomas b 1574 owned Force Smithy, Manor of Hawkshead

moved to Graythwaite, owned Rusland Hall will 16 4 1622 + 1630

= Jane only dau and heiress of John Sawrey of Graythwaite

= Bridget dau John Sawrey of Graythwaite son of Miles Sawrey

Leonard c Hawkshead 1604 of Sandscale + 1652

Henry c Hawkshead 1608

William 1606-80 of Low Graythwaite and Rusland Hall

22 in 1630 Captain William, Captain of militia,

1633 High Constable Furness and Cartmel, buried Hawkshead

cousin John Rawlinson of Hullater

    = 1626 Elizabeth daughter Anthony Sawrey of Plumpton b 1606

        will 1683 died at Rusland

= Hawkshead 1612 Hester dau Adam Sandys = John Sawrey of Plumpton

    Hester inherited Force Smithy

    Mary

 Robert

Richard of Tottlebank in township book Egton cum Newland 1614 will 1647

in will of Robert Rawlinson of Crake 1646

= Elizabeth

    William license for nonconformist worship Tottlebank 1669

    Jannet

    Elizabeth

    Mary

    Margarert = Widdow

    John

    dau = Curwen

        Elizabeth

    dau = Ashburner

        Ann

sister = Richard Holme

sister = William Pennington of Longmire

Elizabeth

Ann

Aunt Gibson

Captain William Rawlinson fought at Marston Moor

Captain William Rawlinson 1606-80 = 1626 Elizabeth Sawrey

Thomas c Hawkshead 1627/8, became a quaker and consequently banned from his fathers house for many years. Small holder and steward of an estate, purchased Force Forge from Fell sisters 1681 }+ Sawrey 1689

= Gleaston Quakers 1663 Dorothy dau Thomas Hutton of Rampside +1737 (93) buried Colthouse Quakers

John b Graythwaite c Hawkshead 1629 of Grays Inn 1688 secretary to the Master of the Rolls, wrote letter to brother Thomas saying that the Princess of Orange had reached Whitehall and that the Prince and she hoped that every house would proclaim them King and Queen,

of Furnivals Inn 1676, of Rusland 1682, entered Gray's Inn 1689, died 1699 will made 1698 proved 1700

= Holy Trinity Minories 1692 Mary Usher

Alice c Hawkshead 1631 =1652 William Thornton of Melling

Giles + 1681 Melling

John c Melling 1663/4

William c Melling 1665

Charles of the Inner Temple

Jane c Hawkshead 1633 +1676 cousin to Madeleine Remington of Hornby

= 1656 Adam Storrs of Storrs Hall 1629-1701/2 b Melling s Henry & Agnes Storrs

Henry c Melling 1662
Anne ca 1633

= Halton Church 1684/5, Charles Cawson

= St Mary, Lancaster 1694 Anthony Askew MD Kendal 1670-1737

Adam MD of Newcastle = Susanna Crackenthorp qv

Anthony of Wakefield

Anthony under 21 in 1737

Margaret = John Fletcher

William c Melling 1668

Elizabeth c Hawkshead 1634/5

= Hawkshead 1657 Luke Pearson of Lingham Yks

      William clerk in Court of Chancery, trustee in Sir Wm Rawlinson's will

          Luke = Alice

      James in London 1680, Rusland 1682

= p 1673 a 1683 William Curwen of Holeslack Helsingham + 1689

Margaret 1635 = 1676 Henry Bateman of The Blease in Old Hutton

Ann c Hawkshead 1637 = Hawkshead, 1662, Richard Chatburn of Hornby

      Margaret c Melling 1664 – affidavit 1683 re gdma Eliz R's funeral

      Thomas c Meling 1667 of 6 clerks office, London 1680

      trustee Sir Wm Rawlinson's will 1703

      Elizabeth

      William c Melling 1670

      Henry Chatburn c Melling 1671

      Richard + 1673/4

Sir William c Hawkshead 1640 Hawkshead School, Christs Cambridge 1655

entered Gray's Inn 1656/7, serjeant at law 1686

of St Andrew Holborn 1686, lived in Chancery Lane, MP for Hendon

commissioner of the Great Seal 1688-1693 with Sir John Maynard & Sir

Anthony Keck

father of the House of Commons, will 1703 + 1703

= 1664 Ann Palmer of Winthorp, Lincolnshire sister in law John Sharp

                            Abp York

      Elizabeth Ann of St And Holburn, 1687, wed either St Giles in the

      Fields   or St James Clerkenwell by lic William Lowther of Middle

      Temple 29 12 1687

      = 1703 Giles Earle MP 1678-1758 of Eastcourt House Crudwell

          William Rawlinson Earle MP 1727-67 b 1702 + 1774

          = Malmesbury 1730 Susanna White of Little Somerford

             Giles of Beningbrough Hall

                William 1763

                Thomas

> Eleanor
>> Eleanor
> Ann + 1700 = 1694 Rt Hn John Aislaby of Studley
>> William MP of Studley Royal 1700-82, bought Fountains Estate
>> Elizabeth = Charles Allanson

= Jane Nosworthy + 1712 bur Ealing

Mary c Hawkshead 1642 = John Burrows soap boiler Derby

> Isaac 1673-1745 trustee in S Wm Rawlinson's will, barrister at law
> Derby will 1746
>> = 1701 Mary Tempest (28) of Waddoe Cambridge
>>> John Tempest

Rebecca c Hawkshead 1646 + 1731 = 1672 James Towers of Kendal

> John c 1674

daughter Benson in father's will (? wife of Robert Benson of Penrith)

daughter

> John Gregg
> Francis Grigg trustee in Sir William Rawlinson's will

Susan = 1680 John Sawrey of Plumpton

Thomas Rawlinson became a Quaker

Thomas Rawlinson c Hawkshead 1627/8

banned from his father's house for many years,

smallholder and steward of an estate. Purchased Force Forge from the Fell sisters 1681

= Gleaston Quakers 1683 Dorothy + 1737 (93) dau Thomas Hutton of Rampside

> to have Low Wray, bur Colthouse Quakers
> William b 1664 will 1734 + 1736 ? of Brampton
> of Gillthwaiterigg, Skelsmergh 1704, formed Backbarrow Iron Co 1711,
> rebuilt Graythwaite Hall 1718,
>> his estate sued 1748 re will of his cousin Thomas Olliphant of Hampstead
>> = 1688 Margery dau Adam Gouldney of Chippenham bur Hawkshead 1698/9
>> = Swarthmoor Quaker 1701 Mary Willison dau Robert Benson of Carlisle

Abraham b 1666 set up iron forge at Caton

= Sw Q 1695 Elizabeth dau William Beck of Low Wray b Hawkshead 1670

+1737

Sarah 1668- 1758

= Sw Q 1698 George Bowley of Hallthey/ Hutton Hall Caldbeck Cumberland

Thomas

Priscilla

Abigail b Rusland 1671 Q

= Sw Q 17021 John Thompson of Powbank Crook Wd

Isaac b Kendal 1703 – poet to whose book Ebenezer Rawlinson, Isaac

Rawlinson and Abraham Rawlinson Jnr subscribed 1737

cofounder Newcastle Journal with Wm Cuthbert. Isaac was printer and

editor till his   death. Surveyor and mapmaker

+ Q 1775 Northumberland Rd Newcastle

= Rachel Maude sister Warren Maude

Jonathan

Hannah

Hannah Q 1676 Rusland + 1675/6

Elizabeth Q 1680 Colton, in Virginia 1718

Isaac Q 1680 Rusland apprenticed to Henry Gouldney London 1696

Lydia Q 1682 Rusland = Kendal Q 1706/7 Brian Lancaster

Ruth Q 1686 Rusland + 1698 (12)

Daniel ? = 1703 Agnes dau Richard Storrs and widow of James Garnett

William Rawlinson ironmaster 1664-1736

William Rawlinson of Gilthwaiterigg Skelsmergh 1704

formed Backbarrow iron Co 1711

rebuilt Graythwaite Hall 1719

will 1734 + 1736

= 1688 Margery dau Adam Gouldney of Chippenham + 1698/9 Hawkshead

Gouldney 1685 will 1769 Gawthwaite

Thomas b 1689 established iron foundry Invergarry 1727, invented modern kilt. conformed to C/E 1733. 1734 sued brothers Job, William, Gouldney, and

Ebenezer and sisters Jane Harderen, Elizabeth Ormston and Margery Maud plus William Williamson, Robert Chambers, John Wilson and a Sawrey

+ 1737 (48) of Whittington Hall

will 1734 principal creditor Isaac Rawlinson innholder Lancaster

= ? Elizabeth dau John Hudson of Haverbrack +1761

Mary c St Michael Whittington 1721

= John Sunderland 1710-82 of All Hallows Lane London

  Judith c St Michael Whittington 1741

  = there 1765 Edward Grigg of Chamber Hall Oldham

  Thomas 1744-1809 c Whittington 1747

  involved with Ulverston Canal

  = Ann Dickson

  Samuel

William apprenticed 1714 to John Chaytor linen draper Dublin

of Southwark 1717, Backbarrow 1718, running brewery Knaresbrough 1723

of Bigland 1724, purchased Rusland from Uncle Abraham 1733/4

of Bankside St Saviour Southwark 1735 and 1744, of Rusland 1749

will 1760 when of Rusland

= 1723 Mary dau Cornelius Cades of Knaresbrough + a 1732

  Ruth Q Hawkshead 1723 = Rookhow Q 1745 Thomas Vickriss Hyam

    Thomas Rawlinson

    Anna Maria

  Margery = St Brides 1747 Simon Warner coal trader Wapping

    Ann Wapping Q 1748

    = Q 1771 John Harris timber dealer Cannon St

    John Wapping Q 1750

    William Wapping 1751 Q

    Thomas Pilgrim Wapping Q 1752

    Ruth Q 1755 Bermondsey St Mary Mg

    Margaret Q 1757

Pilgrim Q 1761 Bermondsey St Mary Mg

William Kn Q 1725 + 1730

Cornelius Kn Q 1727 + 1727/8 bur Scotton Q

Mary + Scotton 1729

Thomas Kn Q 1730 +1731

= London Q 1732 Mary dau George Oldner of Battersea

William 1736 sold Rusland Hall 1762 to Thomas Walker of Thwaitehead

Alice 1741= John Harrison of London

John Q 1696

Job Q 1697/8 + 1763 bur Q of Lowwood Forge and Furnace 1747,

freeman of Lancaster 1735

= Q Brigflatts Elizabeth Willan + 1763

Hannah + 1707

Mary = ? Peter Wilson (? John Wilson)

Jane = Sw Q 1739 Henry Ardern of Stockport

Elizabeth = Sw Q 1718 Charles Ormston of Hendersyde Kelso

Charles

Jean Elizabeth b 1720 = 1756 John Waldie of Berryhill and Hayhope

George + 1824 Hendersyde

= 1779 Ann dau Jonathan Ormston of Newcastle upon Tyne

John 1781 D L

Mary Jane = Richard Griffiths

Charlotte = 1822 Stephen Easton of Stamford

Jane = Adm George Edward Watts

Robert at school with Sir Walter Scott

Catherine = Q 1793 William Rawlinson of Graythwaite

William

Elizabeth

= Swarthmoor 1701 Mary Willison, widow, dau of Robert Benson of Carlisle

Isaac Q 1704 bur Q 15th July 1704

Ebenezer Cartmel Q 1708. at Dorothy Barnes wedding 1727

1731 subscribed to book of poems by Isaac Thompson with Uncle Isaac and cousin Abraham Rawlinson Jnr

c Kendal Christmas Day 1736

= Cartmel when gt of Dent 1747 Elizabeth Stephenson of Newby Bridge

buried 22 8 1760 Castleton Malew Isle of Man when of Furness Fells

adm to William Cubbon

Margery = Swarthmoor and Hawkshead 1732 William Maud

Abraham Rawlinson of Caton and Hornby 1666-1737

Abraham Rawlinson Sw Q 1666 set up iron forge at Caton

should have inherited Rusland Hall by grandfather's will after death of childless Uncle John + 1698

supplied ore to Backbarrow Co 1712, sold 12 acres of peat moss in Rusland Heights

+ 1737 Manchester will 1737 Hornby Melling

= Sw Q 1695 Elizabeth dau William Beck of Low Wray b Hawkshead 1670 + 1756

    Dorothy b Rusland Q 1696 +Lancaster 1768

    with whom young John Lettsom lodged

      = Yelland Q 1727 William Barnes of Grt Sankey,

          constable, supervisor of highways,
of Cow Lane House, Sankey

    John Q 1698 + 1724 + Leighton buried Yelland

    William b Rusland 1700 + 1710

    Isaac b Rusland Q 1701 of Hornby 1733/4
mercer thereafter of Lancaster

      = Gressingham 1733/4 Mary Carus of Melling + 1747/8

        Elizabeth c St Mary Lancaster 1735

        William c St Mary Lancaster 1735/6

        Carus c St Mary Lancaster 1739/40 + 1740/1

        Dorothy c St Mary Lancaster 1740 + 1740/1

        Lydia c St Mary Lancaster 1740 + 1740/1

        Esther c St Mary Lancaster 1740 + 1740/1

        Sarah c St Mary Lancaster 1741/2 bur 1745

        Isaac c St Mary Lancaster 1741/2 mariner + 1788

          = St Mary Lancaster 1770 Elizabeth Boronskill otp + 1825

Abraham c St Mary, Lancaster 1779

c St Ann, Richmond Sq 1783 + 1835

= Ann

Mary c St Nicholas Liverpool 1806

= St Ann Richmond Sq 1808 Sarah Marshall

Abraham c St Ann, Rchmond Sq 1809

Sarah elder daughter + 1817 (6)

Ellen Mary Ann c St Ann Richmond Sq

+ 1830 only surviving dau

Margaret c St Mary, Lancaster

John Carus c St Mary, Lancaster 1781 will San Domingo 1819

Thomas Walter c St Mary, Lancaster 1783

c St Ann Richmond Sq Liverpool 1783

Esther 1705-77 = Wray Q 1732 Thomas Titley of Warrington

Abraham Q 1709 b Low Hall Kirby merchant Lancaster quaker

Freeman of Lancaster 1736 obtained mining rights Lindal and Dalton 1745

witness to sale of Channon House 1772

accused of having letters of marque on his ships (authorisation by the
government to seize foreign ships and remove their goods) which he denied
1779   will 1780

= Q 1739 Ellen Godsalve

Thomas Hutton Q Swarthmoor 1712 b Kirby

Freeman of Lancaster 1734 + 1769 will 1772

= Lancaster Q 1734 Mary Dillworth

Abraham Rawlinson 1709-80 West India merchant of Lancaster

Abraham Rawlinson = Lancaster Q 1739 Ellen Godsalve

Abigail Q 1740 = 1771 William Lindow of Castle Hall Lancaster

Dorothy Q 1740 + 1741

Henry Q 1741 of Grassyard, Freeman of Lancaster 1759

MP for Liverpool 1780-84 + 1786

= North Shields Quakers 1765 Martha dau Peregrine Tysack of Newcastle

John Q Lancaster 1744 of Newcastle, Freeman of Lancaster 1759

will 1781 merchant Lancaster

= Q 1772 Jane Hodgeson

Abraham Q 1776

William Q Lancaster 1748

Thomas of Yealand b 1752 Freeman of Lancaster 1766

slave trader owned Broom Hall in British Guiana and estates in St Vincent

Grenada, Berbice and Demerara.

Sold Yealand and Burton in Kendal.

Killed October 1802 thrown from a gig near Burton

= 1788 Sarah Cowell + a 1802

    Abraham of Fakenham banker +1829= Emma Chapman

        Thomas Abraham barrister = Ann Copeman

            Abraham George Monk 1853 +1900

        Revd William Chapman c Fakenham 1811 vicar Burwell

            Abraham George Rolfe 1851

        Sarah = Richard Bacon banker

Elizabeth Q 1753

William Beck Q Lancaster 1754 of Manchester

Freeman of Lancaster 1766 + Castleton Isle of Man 1811

= Sarah Drury 1764-1859

    William Henry c St Ann Manchester 1783 will 1856 Grt Marlbrough St

    Charlotte Louise 1785 -1870 = Dr Lathom

    Abraham Stanley c St Ann Manchester 1786

    George Hutton 1785-1856, Captain of the East India Co 56 in 41

    Lambeth 65 in 51 retd major Westmorland Regt b Horsham Sussex

    + St James, bur Leckhampton Gloucestershire 7 1 1856

    Harriet Matilda 1787 -1879 of Cheltenham

    Charles James 1788-1858 + Cheltenham

    Elizabeth Lindow 1791 = William Atkinson

    Alicia Anna 1793-1844 = Andrew Seton Kerr

    Daniel 1801

Abraham Beck Q 1754

Samuel Q 1757 of Manchester, Freeman of Lancaster 1779 + Stafford 1810

= 1784 Sarah dau Charles Chorley

    Mary Tote

    Ellen

    Sarah 1795 + Leck 1832

Henry Rawlinson MP for Liverpool 1741-1786

Henry Rawlinson Q 1741 of Grassyard, Freeman of Lancaster 1759

MP for Liverpool 1780-84 + 1786

= North Shields Quakers 1765 Martha dau Peregrine Tysack of Newcastle

    Ellen Q 1766 + Mch 1791 bur Lancaster St Mary

       = Lancaster St Mary 1790 Revd Gilbert Ainslie, of Hinderwell

       c St Mary Carlisle 1763 + Lisbon, Portugal 1692

Marion Q 1766 = St Mary Lancaster 1790 Robert Hesketh

    Edward Fleetwood

    Robert Fleetwood

    Charles 1804

     Sir Peter Fleetwood Hesketh MP 1800-56

       = 1826 Elizabeth Metcalfe

          Anna Maria

          Peter Louis 1838-80

    Ann Marie = Knollys

Martha Q Hardshaw 1769

Dorothy Q Hardshaw 1770

Elizabeth Q Hardshaw 1774

Harriot Q Hardshaw 1774

Abram Tyzack Q Lancaster 1777

c St Ann Richmond Sq, Liverpool 1781

soon after 1798 sold Grassyards and bought property at Chadlington Oxon

= St George, Hanover Square 1800 Eliza Eudocia Albina Creswick
Henry Lindow Rawlinson later Henry Lindow Lindow Q Lancaster 1777
inherited Fountains and Keaton estates in St Vincent was compensated 1833
for freedom of slaves. Of Lower Slaughter bur All Souls Kensal Green 1848
= 1819 Charlotte Elizabeth Barnard

      Henry William stockbroker + 1887 = Westminster 1867

      Charles Thomas + Hay will 1864

      Louisa Elizabeth = St John Paddington 1856, 3rd Ld Fitzhardinge
Peregrine Park + Q 1780 at 6 months

Abram Tysack Rawlinson

Abram Tysack Rawlinson 1777-1845 of Chadlington Oxfordshire
= St George Hanover Square 1800 Eliza Eudocia Albina Creswick

      Anna Maria 1801

      Eudocia Martha c Bourton on the Water 1802

      Maria 1804 = Chadlington 1838 Brooke Smith JP Bristol 1803-81

            Edward Cuthbert

            Eudocia Maria 1841-1914

            Anna Georgiana 1850-61

Abraham Lindow b Chadlington 1805 solicitor Chipping Norton +1875
will 1879
= 1832 Sarah dau Brooke Smith of Bristol, b St Augustine Bristol + 1869 (70)

            Anna Eudocia c Chipping Norton 1834

            headmistress Altrincham 1911 + 1920

            Abraham Henry c Chipping Norton 1836 + 1837

            Abraham Creswick c Chipping Norton 1838 b Chadlington

            23 in 61 medical student, Chelsea. Mayor, Chipping Norton

            1871-1901 solicitor Chipping Norton, + Huxley Alberta 1910

             = Chelsea 1867 Laura Elizabeth A Farwell b Stoke Fleming

            + CN 1886 (46)

            Abraham Leonard c Chipping Norton 1868,

            All Sts School Bloxham 1881

= St Mary Calgary 1908 Emma Tuma

Arthur Creswick c+ 1870

Maude Susanna c Chipping Norton 1870 + 1941 (70)

= Chipping Norton 1899 William Rees Williams of Colwyn Bay

Pauline Marion c Chipping Norton 1872 + 1887

Hester Violet c Chipping Norton 1873 + 1952

Ruby Elma c Chipping Norton 1878

= Chipping Norton 1897 Rev Vincent William Lucas

Ivy Constance Sarah c Chipping Norton 1878 + 1916 (39)

= Chipping Norton 1901 Samuel Walker Gillam of Bath

= Chipping Norton 1890 Frances Amelia Barton + 1922 (83) b Brixton

Georgiana 1806 = Revd Lewis William Heath, vicar Newland

Caroline c Chadlington 1808

Henry Creswick c Chadlington 1810 East India Co, Consul Baghdad

Behuistan Inscription, cuneiform script, Agent at Kandahar MP, 1st Bt +1895

= St George Hanover Square 1862 Louisa Caroline Harcourt Seymour

George b1812 + 1902

Fellow Exeter College, Oxford, Bampton Lecturer, Prof Ancient History

Canon of Canterbury Cathedral

= 1846 Susan Louisa Chermside b France

Edward Augustus b Chadlington 1815 surgeon will 1857 Cleve Somerset

= Westbury on Trim 1841 Susanna Jane 36 in 51 dau Sir Cuthbert Sharpe

Edward Cuthbert Brookes 8 in 51 b Clifton,7th Bengal Cavalry

Deputy Chief Constable Manchester 1881 + Upton Bucks 1890 (48)

= Hove Dt 1875 Louisa Laura Fraser

Henry 4 in 81 b Brighton

Hugh Augustus b Clifton 1878 with Aunt Ellen Gordon 81

Plumstead School,TCC, Wells Theological College 01

missionary Rangoon, vicar Chollerton & Hexham

+ Hampstead 1951 (77)

Irene Louisa b 1887 + 1937

= St Peter in the East Oxford 1909 Burnett Hillard Streeter

biblical scholar Provost Queens College Oxford
author "The Four Gospels" = 1937

Augustus
Henry Augustus c St Pancras 1846+ 1847

Sir Henry Creswick Rawlinson MP 1810-95

Henry Creswick Rawlinson c Chadlington 1810 East India Co, Consul Baghdad
Behuistan Inscription, cuneiform script, Agent at Kandahar, MP, 1st Bt +1895
= St George Hanover Square 1862 Louisa Caroline Harcourt Seymour
Henry Seymour c St Mark Audley St 1864,
General in WWI succesful at Battle of Amiens, 1st Ld Rawlinson 2nd Bt
= Meredith Kenard
Sir Alfred 3rd Bt c St Mark Audley St 1867 = Margaret Greenfield
Sir Alfred 4th Bt

Revd Professor George Rawlinson 1812-1902

George Rawlinson b Chadlington 1812 in Oxford 1841-71, fellow of Exeter,
Bampton Lecturer, Professor of Ancient History, of Tavistock Square 1891
Canon of Canterbury Cathedral + 1902
= 1846 Susan Louisa Chermside b France
Alice Georgiana 13 in 61 b Merton
George Ernest b Oxford 1848, Medical practitioner 1891 + Blean 1891
Mary Louisa 11 in 1861
Maud 2m in 51 b Oxford
Ethel E 15 in 71
Edward Creswick Scott c St Mary Mag Oxford 1859
Charterhouse School 71, Keble, 1877 drowned in the Cherwell 1880 (20)
Sister Louise Helen 1861-1953
Lionel Seymour 1864 Lancing 81, Oxford 82 no college
farmer Augusta Virginia 1910, Staunton Virginia 1930
+ Augusta 1936 bur Thornrose
= Anna Eliza Cochran 70 in 1930 b Virginia
Elizabeth Seymour 29 in 1930

Charles Brooke b 1867 c St Mary Mag Oxford 1868. Lt Col Indian Army
Deputy Commissioner Punjab
= Blean, Kent !891 Wilhelmina Cruikshank Forester
        Eva 8 in 01 = HT Sloan Sq 1927 (20) Bradner Wells Lee
Margaret = Hilton
= St Mary Magdalen, Oxford 1888 Robert Birch Harrison, Clk Stoke Bishop

Thomas Hutton Rawlinson, sea captain, slave trader, West India Trader Lancaster

Thomas Hutton Rawlinson b Kirby Hall Q 1712 Freeman of Lancaster 1734
+ 1769 will 1772
= Lancaster Q 1734 Mary Dilworth
Sarah Q 1735 = Lancaster Q 1735 John Chorley of Rainhill
      Sarah 1774-1852 = John Walker 1736-1864
            Isaac
            Edward
            John
            Elizabeth
            Helen
            Charles Chorley
            Sarah
            Lydia Rawlinson = Revd Thomas Sale vicar Sheffield
      Mary = John Ford
Elizabeth Q 1735
= Lancaster Q 1759 Isaac Ford b Stafford 1728 of M/C +1799
      John = Mary Chorley
            Sally 1784
            John Chorley 1786
            John 1789 -1819Morecambe Lodge Yealand Conyers
            = Elizabeth Lawson
                Abraham Rawlinson Ford 1813-49 JP 1838
                will 1849 Ellel Hall

Mary Elizabeth

= Weld Chapel Southgate 1841 Francis Walker

Robert Rawlinson + 1840

William 1816-98 c St Mary Lancaster 1822

of Rampside 1849 of Ellel Hall 1861, 1871

= 1852 Louisa Ross

Sarah = Charles Walker of New Lanark

= Yealand 1800 Mary dau John Lawson of Lancaster

Elizabeth Sarah 1803

Hutton Rawlinson 1804 worsted weaver Hareholme Whalley

Charles 1806-80 worsted weaver

Robert Hutton 1808 solicitor Adel

= Hannah dau Thomas Benson Pease

John Rawlinson of Morecambe Park 1844-1934

b Leeds, co-editor "History of Warton"

silk manufacturer Bentham,   LLD solicitor, poet,

donated family manuscripts to Lancaster Museum

= St George Bloomsbury 1877 Helen Cordelia Coxhead

Thomas Benson Pease

George Lawson solicitor 1883-1963

= Margaret Ellen

Margaret Clara Benson = Arthur S Raple

Ursula Ormiston

Mary

Isabel Ormiston

Hannah Q 1735 = Robert Barclay

Abraham Rawlinson Barclay 1794-1845

Mary Q 1737-38

Abraham Q 1738 slaver of Ellel Hall, dismembered by Quakers 1779

c St Mary Lancaster 1680 as adult ex Quaker MP for Lancaster

+ 1803 will 1804

= Shotton Q 1766 Ann Dodgson dau Robert Dodgson of Shildon Durham

Cecilia Q 1740-1 + 1741

John 1741-89 Freeman of Lancaster 1759

= Shotton Q 1766 Mary Heighington will 1812

    Thomas Hutton Q Lancaster 1767 Freeman of Lancaster 1782/3

    + 1787

    John 1770-1772

    Lydia will 1798 at 52

    Thomas Hutton Freeman of Lancaster 1766

    = Lancaster Q 1766 Hannah Satterthwaite

    Mary Hutton 1779 = St Mary, Lancaster 1790 Sir Vyall Vyvyan 7th Bt

        Sir Richard Rawlinsin Vyvyan, MP 8th Bt 1800-79

    Dilworth Q Lancaster 1754 + 1761

Elizabeth

Job Rawlinson of Graythwaite 1697/8 -1763

Job Rawlinson of Graythwaite Q 1697 Freeman of Lancaster 1735

Lowood Forge and Furnace 1747 and fff will 1757 bur Q 1763

= Q Brigflatts 1736 Elizabeth Willan + 1768

    Margery Q 1736

    Lydia Maria Q 1738

    William Q 1740 Freeman of Lancaster 1767 + 1808

    = Q 1793 Catherine dau John Waldie of Hendersyke

        William Q 1794 + 1815

        John Job Q 1798 + 1864 (66) bur Hawkshead,

        Trinity College, Cambridge, built Graythwaite New Hall 1820

        Freeman of Lancaster 1826, of Graythwaite and Duddon Hall till 1864

        63 in 1861 barrister at law, assistant tythe enclosure commissioner

        = Colton 1831 Mary 1808-90 dau John Romney of Whitestock Hall Ulverston

            Catherine Jane c Hawkshead 1832

            = Bootle 1860 Cpt Archibald John Oliver Rutherford

            Edith Elizabeth c Hawkshead 1833, 56 in 91 Portsea

= Bootle 1856 Joseph Stonehewer Scott Chad
of Thursford Hall Norfolk
      1898-1907, High Sheriff of Norfolk
Charles 1856 = Alice Pares
      Cecil Alice = Gerald Duckworth publisher
Cecilia Catherine c Thurford 1868 + 1968
= Thurford 1892 Charles Russell Day
Mary c Thurford 1869
William Sawrey c Hawkshead 1837,
gent cadet Greenwich 1861 at 15
magistrate and landowner, of Duddon Hall,
Major 12th dragoons 1861
of Parkfield, Weston, Somerset 1871
bur St Mary Magdalen Broughton in Furness 1875 (40)
= St George Hanover Square 1862 Elizabeth Mary Brooke of
                    Bath
    William Brooke Millers b Duddon Hall 1863
    school in Cheltenham 1881,Trinity College Cambridge
    visiting John Rawlinson Ford at Morecambe Lodge
    1891   + Ulverston District 1892 (33)
    = St George Hanover Square 1889 Rosetta Ella Rigge
        Lt William Gray 1 in 91 + St Eloi France 1915
        executor of uncle GBM Rawlinson 1913
    George Brookes Millers b Duddon Hall 1864
    army camp Pembroke 1891, retd army major
    Broughton Bank Lower Allithwaite 1911
    + High Duddon 1913 (49) will 1916
    Robert Henry Millers b Duddon Hamm 1865,
    Downing Coll Cambridge 1886,
    homestead grant Alberta 1888
        George Henry 1891-1962 bur Calgary
        = Susanna Readham 1894-1986

Virginia Flora 1912-2002

= Alban Bruce Ross

Kenneth Henry 1920-1935 bur Calgary

Arthur Millers b Kents Bank 1866 went to Alberta

+ 1926

Hackney Horse breeder Bowe River Alberta,
near Calgary, rum manufacturer Barbados 1907-1909

Thomas b Bootle District 1867

Christopher Millers b Weston Bath District 1869

hackney horse breeder Bowe River Alberta

rum manufacturer Barbados 1907-1909

+ Calgary Alberta 1942

Alice Millers b Rottingdean Sussex 1873 +m 1951

of Lower Allithwaite 1911

= St George, Hanover Sq District 1897

 John Herbert Cadogan of Bath

 Lt Col Roger John Edward Cadogan- Rawlinson

 b 1873 lead military campaign in Hong Kong

 +1951

 = a 1932 Moya McGreevor McDonell

  Kenneth Roger Brook 1931-2008

  commander

  = 1959 Rosemary E Stock

   John Edward b Plymouth 1964

   = Victoria

  Christopher Robert Johnstone 1936-2010

  of Brampton Norfolk

  = Margaret E Birley

   Timothy S b Norwich 1960

   Joanna 1967

   Michael Simon 1969

  = Wilhelmina de Kuyper

Isabella = Alstone

= Mary Jane Easton

Martin Lloyd 1945

George Romney b Milnthorp c Hawkshead 1939

4 in 1841 of Low Graythwaite, Harrow School 1851

Army Lt 1861

Colonel 3rd Regt Dragoons + Grt Malvern 1880 (43) will 1880

Robert c Hawkshead 1839, 2 in 41 Low Graythwaite

god child Thomas Alcock Beck of Esthwaite Lodge

Hammersmith School 1851 then Trinity College, Cambridge

of Duddon Hall 1861 and 71, JP 1872 Graythwaite +1889

of Sella Park Cumberland then Graiyhwaite, Cheltenham 1881

= Ulverston 1866 Eleanor Jane dau Rev John Baldwin

vicar of Dalton in Furness

widow Cheltenham 1891 and 1901

Robert Rawlinson 1839-1889 of Graythwaite, Duddon Hall and Sella Park

Robert Rawlinson 1839- 1889 + Cheltenham

= Ulverston 1866 Eleanor Jane dau Rev John Baldwin of Dalton in Furness 57 in 01

John Baldwin b St Bridget Bekermet 1867 of Bredfield School, Berks 81 then

Malvern then Brasenose Oxford 1885, blue for cricket,

living with Aunt Edith Chad 91. with wife 01 Hotel Metropole, St Martin in

the Fields, sold Old Graythwaite Hall aka Low Graythwaite Hall and estate

1905, boarding in Babbacombe 1911 and Worthing 1939 separated from wife

+ Kensington 1945

= Cheltenham 1893 Theodosia Wilhelmina Stokes + a 1939

sailed to USA from Liverpool 1907 +Dublin

Alice Maud c+ 1893

Robert b 1894 Ulverston District, of Graythtwaite Hall 01

at Tiverton School 1911 2nd Lt killed in action 1915

Marjorie Vera b Cheltenham 1896 of Graythwaite Old Hall 1901
later lived with grandmother Maria Stokes
= Bombay 1924 Gp Capt Frederick Lawrence 9 3 1898 + 22 11 19xx
Revd Gerald Christopher c St Bridget Bekermet 1868 of Graythwaite 1871
in Cheltenham 81, Exeter College, Oxford 1868 ex Malvern, living with
mother 91, curate Wymering Hants 1901, curate St Barnabas Pimlico 1911and
fff,visited USA and West Indies, + Holborn House Pimlico 1920 (37)
monument in St Barnabas Church, will adm to sister Eleanor Maud
Eleanor Maud c Hawkshead 1871 lived with mother in Cheltenham
Evelyn b Graythwaite c Hawkshead 1874 + 1919
= Cheltenham 1897 John Fell Woodbourne of Geenodd
Cuthbert Aislabie b Cheltenham 1881 schood in Bedford 1901
patient Teddington Hospital 1911 +Staines 1942
Constance Mary b Cheltenham 1884
Leonard Hugh b Cheltenham 1888
Lt Longmore Army Camp East Liss Hants 1911 + 1915

LONG PEDIGREE OF RAWLINSON OF GRIZEDALE, MARSH GRANGE FENHURCH ST ETC

Robert Rawlinson held land Hawkshead 1538

Robert Rawlinson + Hawkshead 1568 subsidy roll 1598

    Thomas b 1520 will 1591

    = Margaret will 1594/5 sister Richard Otley and Charles Otley

        Robert of Grizedale b 1560 will 1606/09

        = Elizabeth dau Thomas Hutton of Thorpinsty +1627

            Thomas fl 1627 qv

            = Hawkshead 1608 Susanna Steinberger (Stonehewer in

                register) granddaughter Daniel Hochstetter of
Keswick

            John of Hullater will 1647 = f + Colton 1637

            Margaret

            Robert to inherit Colton + a 1632

            = Ann = a 1632 John Ambrose of Lowick

            Ann

            Susanna = Hawkshead 1623 George Browne of Troutbeck

    Thomas

    Leonard

        Thomas

        William

        Ann

    Mrs Fox

    Leonard 1550-99 court steward of Low Furness under Q Elizabeth
surveyed Borrowdale for the crown, sub roll 1581 1598 Dalton
of Angerton Moss and Broughton Tower

    = St Mary Dalton in Furness 1568 Agnes Richardson +1612

    John 1571 of Sandscale will 1640 = Elizabeth (? Gurnell of Millom)

= Dalton 1608 Grace Bolton

      Leonard c Dalton 1609 of Broughton Tower

      = ? Hawkshead 1629 Mary Wright +1636

            Robert c Hawkshead 1631/2

            children

      = Elizabeth

      John c Dalton 1613

            Charles c Dalton 1647/8

            Margaret c Dalton 1651/2

            Elizabeth c Dalton 1652

            Richard c Dalton 1653 +1699

            servant Thomas Richardson of Roanhead

            = Lic 1682 Mary Knipe

                  = Aldingham 1710 Thomas Richardson

            Hester c Dalton 1656

            William c Dalton 1659

      Robert c Dalton 1614

      Elizabeth c Dalton 1615/6

      Charles c Dalton 1617

      Cornelius c Dalton 1619

      Isabel c Dalton 1622

Thomas 1574

      Leonard c Hawkshead 1604

= Hawkshead 1612 Hester Sands

      Jane c+ 1613

      Leonard c Hawkshead 1615

      Samuel c Hawkshead 1621 + 1623

      Hester

      Ann

      Janet

= Hawkshead 1622 Janet Sands

Robert 1577 of Marsh Grange = Margaret = John Kirkby

William 1582

Richard 1587

Sawrey

Agnes

Thomas Rawlinson of Grizedale

Thomas Rawlinson of Grizedale

= Hawkshead 1608 Susanna Steinberger

    Thomas 1609-54 apprentice to brother Daniel 1650 bur Hawkshead

    Robert c Hawkshead 1612/3 + a 1667 qv

    Daniel c Hawkshead 1614/5 apprenticed to Ellen S vintner

    vintner of London, The Mitre Fenchurch St. friend Samuel Pepys

    helped rebuild Hawkshead School and Satterthwaite Chapel of Ease

    cousin to William Rawlinson of Grays Inn (of Graythwaite family) and John

    Rawlinson of Hullatter +a 1679 MI St Dionis Backchurch

    =St George the Martyr Southwark 1637 Margaret Paviour

    Susanna c Hawkshead 1617

    Radegunda c Hawkshead 1618

    Hester c Hawkshead 1618

    Samuel 1621-1623

    Elizabeth c Hawkshead 1625/6

        = Jones

        = Hamlet Evans clerk Middleton bur St Leonard Middleton 13 1 1660/1

            Thomas vintner London living with Uncle Daniel 1644

            apprenticed 1661 to Daniel Rawlinson vintner

            = Mary bur 1669 St Dionis Backchurch

            John

            Ann = Butterworth

Robert Rawlinson c 1612/32

Robert Rawlinson c Hawkshead 1612/3 +a 1667

Dorothy c Hawkshead 1634 = Postlethwaite

Ann c Hawkshead 1635/6

Jane c Hawkshead 1637/8 = Hawkshead 1656 James Frearson

      Dorothy c Hawkshead 1658 b Grizedale

      Ellen c Hawkshead 1659/60 b Grizedale

      Jane c Hawkshead 1662 b Grizedale

      Robert c Hawkshead 1665 b Grizedale

      John c Hawkshead 1667 b Grizedale

      Thomas c Hawkshead 1672 b Grizedale

      Mary c Hawkshead 1674/5 b Grizedale

Elizabeth c Hawkshead 1640

Mary c Hawkshead 1641 = Hawkshead 1676 Thomas Borwick

Thomas c Hawkshead 1643 + 1643

Thomas c Hawkshead 1644 + 1646

Daniel c Hawkshead 1645 + 1647

Susanna c Hawkshead 1647

= Hawkshead 1681 Adam Ashburner of Greenodd

      William c Hawkshead 1681

 Daniel c Hawkshead 1654 will 1701 apprenticed to John Billingsley vintner

1673   + vintner St Mary Newington qv

= Elizabeth Billingsley b 1653 buried Reigate 21 4 1721 will

Robert distiller apprenticed 1667 to Daniel Rawlinson vintner the Mitre

= Mary daughter Sir Thomas Bashfield

      Daniel c St John Wapping 1676 (7 in 1680)

      + 1701 on ship "Ruby" bound for East Indies

      Thomas apprenticed 1693 to John Brown vintner

      possibly cousin to Dame Elizabeth Sanderson

      = Margaret Woolred (both fl 1738)

            Margaret in will Elizabeth Rawlinson of Reigate 1715

            Elizabeth

Daniel Rawlinson 1654-1701

Daniel Rawlinson c Hawkshead 1654

will 1701 + vintner St Mary Newington

= Elizabeth Billingsley b 1653 buried Reigate 1721 will

    Daniel c St Martin Ongar died Reigate

    = St Mary Reigate 1726 Deborah Jones will 1746/8

        Daniel buried St Giles in the Fields 1731

    Robert c St Dionis Backchurch 1680

    rector of Charlwood 1711-47 will 1747 bur St Dionis Backchurch 1747

    = Denham 1705 Margaret dau Richard Ray of Cambridge +1714

        Daniel c St Alphege Greenwich 1709

        Daniel c St Nicholas Charlwood 1713

        trustee sister Mary's marriage settlement 1736

        Sir Thomas Lord Mayor of London + 1769

        partner Rawlinson and Davison tea merchants

        = St James Garlickhythe 1734 Dorothy + 1761 dau Rev Richard Ray

            Sir Walter MP 1734-1805 of Inner Temple 1769

            c All Hallows Staining 1735

            of Ladbroke and Rawlinson bankers

            = St James North Cray 1769 Mary Ladbroke

            Theodosia c All Hallows Staining 1736

            Thomas c All Hallows Staining 1737

            Richard c All Hallows Staining 1743

            Susanna = Sir George Wombwell 1st BT

        Revd Robert TCC 1723 bur Charlwood 1737

        Richard

    = St Andrew Holborn 1715 Mary dau Thomas Manningham Bp of Chichester will 1752

        Mary = St Katherine Coleman 1736 Francis Ellis woollen warper

                     Cornhill London will 1765/72

        Robert c St Michael Cornhill 1737

        Mary c St Michael Cornhill 1738

Catherine c St Michael Cornhill 1740

Mary c St Michael Cornhill 1742

Francis c St Michael Cornhill 1743

Francis c St Michael Cornhill 1744

Anna Maria c St Michael Cornhill 1745/6

William c St Michael Cornhill 1747

Henry c St Michael Cornhill 1748

William c St Michael Cornhill 1749

Daniel Rawlinson 1614/5- a 1679 of The Mitre Fenchurch St

Daniel Rawlinson c Hawkshead 1614/5 apprenticed to Ellen Spillman vintner 1634

of the Mitre Fenchurch St, friend of Samuel Pepys, helped with rebuilding Hawkshead School, providing a library, rebuilding Satterthwaite Chapel of Ease

cousin to John Rawlinson of Hullatter and William Rawlinson of Gray's Inn +a 1679

= St George the Martyr Southwark 1637 Margaret Paviour + 1665 of plague

    child buried St Dionis Backchurch 1641

    William c St Dionis Backchurch 1642

    Elizabeth c St Dionis Backchurch 1643 bur St Dionis 1651

    Margaret c St Dionis Backchurch 1645 + Donnington Newbury Berks 1711

    widow of Shaw Berks will

    There was a dispute 1711 between Thomas Cowsland & Thomas

    Rawlinson re-her personal estate at Shaw

     = St Olave Hart St 1672 John Honnour 1634-79 will 1680 Hadley

        Margaret

    = St Martin Outchurch 1696/7 Joseph Cowslad +1709/0

    will 1709 Donnington

    Sir Thomas c St Dionis Backchurch 1647, apprenticed to father 1663 + 1708

    will

    Ld Mayor of London land in Grisedale, Essex Surrey and Wasperton Wwks

    = L St Dunstan in the West 1680 Mary Taylor who remarried Stephen

    Hutchinson and Michael Lister of Burwell Lincs

    John c St Dionis Backchurch 1648 will 1689/96 vintner

Maria c St Dionis Backchurch 1650 + 1669

= St Dionis Backchurch 1678 Sir John Mazine of St Martins in the Fields
+1705

Rawlinson + St Dionis Backchurch 1678

Elizabeth c St Dionis Backchurch 1651

Sir Thomas Rawlinson 1647-1708 = St Dunstan in the West 1680 Mary Taylor

Samuel + St Dionis Backchurch 1674 father distiller

Thomas c St Sepulchre Holburn 1681 matriculated Oxford 1698 (19) barrister

obsessive book collector, bankrupted by South Sea Bubble

bur St Botolph Aldgate 1725/ 6 will 1725/6

= 1724 Amy Frewen remarried St Paul's Cathedral 1725 John Tabor

Anna Maria c St Sepulchre, Holburn 1682 bur St Dionis Backchurch 1687

Daniel c St Sepulchre Holburn 1683 bur St Dionis Backchurch 1686

Mary c St Sepulchre Holburn 1685 bur St Dionis Backchurch 1685

Margaret c St Sepulchre Holburn 1686

Daniel c St James Garlickhythe 1687

merchant wine cooper Crutched Friars will 1747

bur St Dionis Backchurch 1747

= St Swithin, London Stone, 1702 Rebecca King

Rebecca c St Dionis Backchurch 1703 bur St Dionis Backchurch 1704

divorced Rebecca for adultery 1706. she buried St Giles Cripplegate 1723

Crutched Friars

= St Michael Cornhill 1740 Elizabeth Davies when both of St Olave Hart St.

when Daniel's widow had a law suit with Adrian

Watkins wine cooper

Susanna Maria c St Sepulchre Holburn 1688 bur St Dionis Backchurch 1700

Richard 4th son 1690-1755 antiquarian book collector,

(collection now in the Bodlian Library and the Ashmoleum Museum),

founded Anglo-Saxon Professorship Oxford, heart in a memorial in St John's

College Chapel Oxford. A non juror bishop

left money to Elizabeth wife of John Markham

Constantine 1692 -1770 lived at Venice, visited there by Walter Rawlinson
MP

William c St Sepulchre Holburn 1693 + Antwerp 1732

= Ann Johnson

    Thomas c St Sepulchre Holburn 1718 slave trader + Antihua 1749

    = Sefton 1738 Rachel Hythe of Liverpool & Ashton under Lyne +1781

        wed as widow Aul Robert Colshed attorney

        Richard c + St Peter Liverpool 1740

        Catherine c St Peter 1741 died same day

        Ann c St Peter 1743 b Cable St

        = St Nicholas 1766 John Williams joiner

        Honour c St Peter 1744 b Pool Lane

        = St George 1765 Robert Kewley cooper

            Ellen c St Peter 1766 bur St James Toxteth 1813 spinster

            William c + St Peter 1768

            Thomas c St Peter 1768 + St Peter 1771

            Mary c St Peter 1770 + St Peter 1772

            Elizabeth c St Peter 1773 bur St James Toxteth 1799

            spinster

            Lee c St Peter 1771 + St Peter 1777

            Robert c St Peter 1777 + St Peter 1778

            Mary c St Peter 1780 + St Peter 1797

            Thomas c St Nicholas 1781 + St Nicholas 1786

            John c St Nicholas 1788 + St Nicholas 1789

        Dorothy c St Peter 1745/6

        = St Nicholas 1763 James Berkley Bur St Peter 1782 smith

            Tarleton St

            Rawlinson c St Peter 1774, bur St Peter 1775

            William c St Peter 1778 bur St Peter 1778

        Ellen c St Peter 1748

    Mary Ann c 1719

    Honour 1721

Susanna Maria c St James Piccadilly 1725

Ann c St Sepulchre Holburn 1694 +1768

= Robert Andrews dry salter

      Honour c 1732 = ? Stoughton Clark

      given copy of "Crys of London" by uncle Tempest Rawlinson 20 7 1734

      Ann c 1734

Honour 1695 - 1751 = John Starke of East India Co

John ca 1697 matriculated Corpus Christi, Oxford 1713 at 15 degree 1718

army officer, bankrupt died at Little Leigh Cheshire 9 1 1753

Tempest c St Sepulchre Holborn 1701

apprenticed to Robert Andrews brother in law

of 16 Cheyne Row 1725-36 following Lady Mary Rawlinson 1717-25

bur St Dionis Backchurch 1736/7

Mary unm 1755

Robert Rawlinson of Grizedale = Elizabeth Hutton

      Thomas = Susan Steinberger

      John of Hullater will 1647 = wife + Colton 1637

            Margaret

            = Colton 1638/9 Richard Rawlinson of New Close 1651/61

            John + Hullater 1686

            = Elizabeth + 1688 dau Thomas Fletcher of Ravenswinder

                  John c Colton 1651

                        Elizabeth c Colton 1681

                        John c Colton 1681

                William c Colton 1626

                Jane

                Elizabeth

                Thomas c Colton 1630 of Hullater

                      William c Colton 1677 of Hullater

                            Job c Colton 1792

                      Thomas c Colton 1679/80 of Kent St,

                    Southwark 1702

Mary c Colton 1631//2

Katherine c Colton 1634

Daniel

Richard Rawlinson of New Close will 1651/61

dispute re Stricklandclose with John Rawlinson of Hullater

= Colton 1638/9 Margaret Rawlinson of Hullater

      Richard

      Elizabeth

      Agnes

Agnes = Colton 1641 Thomas Gaitskell of Little Urswick

      Richard c Urswick 1643

      Robert c Urswick 1645

      Frances c Urswick 1649

      Marie c Urswick 1650

      Eals (m) c Urswick1652

Rawlinson = Eliza will 1797 widow Hullater

Mary = Dalton in Furness 1684 Thomas Kellet of Kringlemire

      Grace = Colton 1688 Robert Rigg

      Rebecca = Colton 1689 Robert Walker

          John c Colton 1690 b Hullater

          Elizabeth c Colton 1692

John Rawlinson of Hullater will 1687 adm John Rawlinson of Hullater, William Rawlinson of Whitieshaw Furness Fells, John Rawlinson of Grizedale and Richard Rawlinson of New Close yeomen trustees Mr Robert Rawlinson, William Rawlinson, Robert Rawlinson, Richard Rawlinson

BIBLIOGRAPHY

Marjoleine Karrs "Blood on the River" 1763 Slave Rebellion Berbice Dutch Guyana

Anna Keay "The Restless Republic – Britain without a crown"

Clare Hickman " The Doctors Garden " John Ledsome and others

Melinda Elder "The Slave Trade"

Melinda Elder " Lancaster and the African Slave Trade"

Margarette Lincoln "London in the 17th Century"

Owen Rutter "At the Three Sugar Loaves and Crown " Davison Newman and Company

Anne C Parknson "Catholicism in the Furness Penisula 1127-1997

Mike Derbyshire " Introductory Guide to the Records of the Palatine of Lancaster"

Sir Henry Slingsby "Diary of Sir Henry Slingsby"

Robert David, Michael Winstanley with Margaret Bainbridge "The West Indies and the Artic in the age of sail – The voyages of Abram 1806-62"

George W Paulsen MD " William Thornton MD a gentleman of the enlightenment"

Arthur Raistrick "Quakers in Science and Industry"

John Miller "The English Civil Wars"

Jeremy Black "Slavery"

Malcolm Balen "A very English Deceit" South Sea Company

David Cooke "The Civil War in Yorkshire"

David Cooke "The Road to Marston Moor"

Peter Earle "The Making of the English Middle Class- London 1660-1730"

Hester Grant "The Good Sharpes"

Richard Lee Bradshaw " God,s Battleaxe" Richard Bradshaw the regicide

Anne Crawford " The History of the Vintner's Company"

A E Rooks "The Black Joke" an anti slavery ship in the West Africa Squadron

M F Thomas " A History of Tottlebank Baptist Church"

Foster Sunderland " A brief History of Tottlebank Baptist Church"

Richard Hoyle "Tudor Taxation Records"

Georgiana Rawlinson Tashjian, David R Tashjian & Brian J Enright " Richard Rawlinson – a Tercentenary Perspective"

Rusland Heritage Trust "Whats in a Name?"

Lynette Cunliffe "The Rawlinsons of Furness Fells"

SOURCES

Most of the wills used are either at the Lancashire Record Office at Preston or Prerogative Court of Canterbury available on Ancestry and at Kew. Lancashire Record Office also hold a fair number of deeds, letter collections, business archives as does the Barrow Record Office with some also at Carlisle Record Office and at the Greater London Record Office and the Guildhall library. Further papers are at St John's College Oxford, Oxford University Archives and The Bodleian. Google Advanced produced a number of incidental facts like Tempest Rawlinson's gift of "London Cries" to his niece Honour. Mention has been made of the books donated to Hawkshead Grammar School and still housed in the same building now a museum, which were donated by Daniel Rawlinson and others. A number of them have informative bookplates

Printed in Great Britain
by Amazon

41139342R00086